From Post-Intersectionality to Black Decolonial Feminism

T0384946

In this accessible and yet challenging work, Shirley Anne Tate engages with race and gender intersectionality, connecting through to affect theory, to develop a Black decolonial feminist analysis of global anti-Blackness.

Through the focus on skin, Tate provides a groundwork of historical context and theoretical framing to engage more contemporary examples of racist constructions of Blackness and Black bodies. Examining the history of intersectionality including its present 'post-intersectionality', the book continues intersectionality's racialized gender critique by developing a Black decolonial feminist approach to cultural readings of Black skin's consumption, racism within 'body beauty institutions' (e.g. modelling, advertising, beauty pageants) and cultural representations, as well as the affects which keep anti-Blackness in play.

This book is suitable for undergraduate and postgraduate students in gender studies, sociology and media studies.

Shirley Anne Tate is Professor and Canada Research Chair Tier 1 in Feminism and Intersectionality, Sociology Department, University of Alberta and Honorary Professor, Nelson Mandela University. Being an African-descent Jamaican impacts her research on Black diaspora studies, the intersections of race and gender, institutional racism, Blackness, affect, 'race' performativity and Caribbean decolonial theory.

Gender Insights

Queer Theories: An Introduction
From Mario Mieli to the Antisocial Turn
Lorenzo Bernini

Objectification
On the Difference between Sex and Sexism
Feona Attwood, Alan McKee, John Mercer, Susanna Paasonen and Clarissa Smith

From Post-Intersectionality to Black Decolonial Feminism
Black Skin Affections
Shirley Anne Tate

https://www.routledge.com/Gender-Insights/book-series/GendIn

From Post-Intersectionality to Black Decolonial Feminism

Black Skin Affections

Shirley Anne Tate

LONDON AND NEW YORK

Designed cover image: lucafabbian, iStock /Getty Images Plus, #494094443

First published 2023
by Routledge
4 Park Square, Milton Park, Abingdon, Oxon OX14 4RN

and by Routledge
605 Third Avenue, New York, NY 10158

Routledge is an imprint of the Taylor & Francis Group, an informa business

British Library Cataloguing-in-Publication Data
A catalogue record for this book is available from the British Library

Library of Congress Cataloging-in-Publication Data
Names: Tate, Shirley Anne, author.
Title: From post-intersectionality to Black decolonial feminism : black skin affections / Shirley Anne Tate.
Identifiers: LCCN 2022027718 (print) | LCCN 2022027719 (ebook) | ISBN 9780367675660 (hardback) | ISBN 9780367674946 (library binding) | ISBN 9781003131823 (ebook)
Subjects: LCSH: Racism. | Black race--Color. | Colorism. | Women, Black. | Sexism. | Feminist theory.
Classification: LCC HT1521 .T383 2023 (print) | LCC HT1521 (ebook) | DDC 305.8--dc23/eng/20220722
LC record available at https://lccn.loc.gov/2022027718
LC ebook record available at https://lccn.loc.gov/2022027719

ISBN: 978-0-367-67566-0 (hbk)
ISBN: 978-0-367-67494-6 (pbk)
ISBN: 978-1-003-13182-3 (ebk)

DOI: 10.4324/b23223

Typeset in Bembo
by SPi Technologies India Pvt Ltd (Straive)

Contents

Figures

Acknowledgements

I could not have written this book without the love and support of my family – Encarna, Soraya, Damian, Jenna, Tev'ian, Lachlan, Arion, Nolan, QT and Shaon. Lots of love to you all.

Parts of the discussion in Chapter 4 appeared in my chapter 'Border Bodies: Mixedness and Passing in *Prison Break*'. In M. Grzinic (2018) (ed.) *Border Thinking: Disassembling Histories of Racial Violence*. Vienna: Sternberg Press. pp. 138–151.

For my late colleague, comrade and mentor Ian Law (2022) who understood there will always be intersectional antiracist work to do.

1 Black skin affections

Black feminist decolonial reading into freedom

Introduction: Skin, flesh, body

I look at picture after picture in the newspaper in 2020 as Covid-19 takes its toll on Black lives in the UK. It seems odd that no-one but other Black people remark that we are dying in disproportionate amounts to our numbers in the population. All I can do at that point is cry, grieve for people unknown, people who I will never know. They are gone. Picture after picture in the *Guardian* remind me of Black vulnerability, Black deaths from a new disease, made worse by structural/institutional racial inequality. Doctors, nurses, care workers, taxi drivers, cleaners, ticket attendants, families, ripped apart by grief and loss. Now they paint hearts on a wall near Westminster in the UK to mark the losses. In the US and UK, they have had a national day of remembrance. Nothing makes it better, as we see in the video #you clap for me now. Too many Black lives have been lost. Now join this grief to George Floyd's murder at white police hands, on impossible to watch viral repeat, and the grief over-flows into mourning, complaint, uprising stirred by anger, pain and an unwillingness to give in to Black negation and violation which would contain Black women, children and men within coloniality's 'flesh' irrespective of skin tone. This is Hortense Spillers' (2003) flesh, and it seems important to me to remember now because it brings back the fact that we are still not free, Black skin marks the body as still just flesh, non-human, non-citizen, un-grievable. For Frank Moten (2018: 245), someday 'it will

DOI: 10.4324/b23223-1

be really important to get at the precisely unlocatable difference between skin and flesh, between Fanon and Spillers'. Covid-19 and George Floyd/Breonna Taylor and so many others, mean this someday is long past. I will attempt to attend to Moten's 'unlocatable difference' in this book to try and find a space to talk about Blackness in an anti-Black world by thinking through flesh, body and its surfacing, what covers it. Skin.

Death,
Loss,
Grief,

haunt Western Hemispheric Black experience. Here, anti-Blackness is set within contemporary coloniality's narrative, joining its constructions of Black flesh to 21st-century Black bodies. As we saw with #BLM 2020, Black bodies do have affective lives in the 21st century, even when they no longer breathe. Even when they have died. Even when they are reduced to flesh in Western Hemispheric death worlds (Mbembe, 2019). Reduced to skin, covering bone, muscles, tendons, ligaments, tissue. Though it is the biggest organ, skin is not just organic matter. *Skin carries meanings. Skin has the capacity to affect and to be affected.* As #BLM 2020 showed us, being affected, *affections*, can lead to *the capacity to affect* through action.

Skin's capacity to affect is linked to its politicization as a hyper-visible marker of race and racialized difference (Mercer, 1994). Anti-Black racism is based on racialized difference read through skin, and through racialization, this difference is constantly being (re)constructed for us by the long arc of coloniality. Colonial skin affections are still alive in the 21st century because Black skin matters in a context where race is political (Roberts, 2011) because skin marks us for life or death. Fred Moten (2018: 242) speaks about the mark of skin as negation, which means that 'Blackness comes into relief against the backdrop of its negation, which takes the form of epidermalization, of a reduction of some to flesh, and the status of no-bodies, so that some others can stake their impossible claim to bodies and souls'.

As no-bodies, as solely flesh, Black deaths through extra-judicial police killings and Covid-19 do not count. This is even the case when race-based data shows the level of carnage, brutality and lost lives due to epidermalization – Black women's, men's, and children's reduction to 'things'. This 'thingification' (Fanon, 2021; Césaire, 2000) has negative affects attached, such as anti-Black hate, contempt, disgust and disdain. These in turn become skin affections that in continually attaching and being attached to Black bodies have led to the Afro-pessimist assertion that people of African descent in the Western Hemisphere still live in enslavement's afterlife (cf. Hartman, 1997, 2016; Sexton, 2011; Sharpe, 2010, 2016; Wilderson 111, 2010, 2020).

Moten's aim is to get at the difference between 'skin' and 'flesh' within enslavement's afterlife. What we need to do to meditate on this difference is to look at Black skin's affects/affections as the discursive and systemic glue in the systematic reduction of some to flesh, to no-bodies. Undoubtedly, this reduction has colonial routes and roots, and this is important to recall and keep to the front of our minds. However, I would also like to suggest that negative Black skin affects/affections had a much earlier emergence in the European imagination than this colonial periodization, which would set it at 1492. Or, if we follow Sylvia Wynter (1996), the year shifts to 1444.

Irrespective of periodization, we can trace European anti-Blackness to the Middle Ages (5th–15th century) where Black skin already signified difference and, on the body of women, hyper-sexualization. For example, during the Middle Ages (1119–1142), 'the religious scholar Peter Abelard, wrote to Hélöise on the *Song of Songs* and the Ethiopian, the Queen of Sheba, being chosen for the King's bed, "besides it so happens that the skin of black women, less agreeable to the gaze, is softer to touch and the pleasures one derives from their love are more delicious and delightful" (Sharpley-Whiting, 2007: 1, cited in Tate, 2015a: 18). Thus, from the Middle Ages in Europe, we already see epidermalization (Fanon, 2021; Moten, 2018: 242). Although a Queen, Sheba was reduced to only flesh and her skin to a signifier of hetero-sexualized eroticism and racial gender difference. She had no body, no soul, whilst

Hélöise and Abelard as the pious Christian source of judgement of human worth, became bodies and/with souls. This epidermalization continued and we see it again in the 1400s 'middle passage' from the West coast of Africa to the Mediterranean basin (Spillers, 2003; Buscaglia–Salgado, 2003; King, 2019; Robinson, 2021; Wynter, 1996):

> Gomes Eannes de Azurara, who drafted *The Chronicle of the Discovery and Conquest of Guinea*, reported that in 1441 sailors – perhaps including Antham Gonçalvez – brought back the first Negroes and "gold dust" to Portugal [...] the 1440s mark the commencement of the Portuguese slave trade, as well as European voyages poised for the conquest of territory on the coast of Africa.
>
> (King, 2019: 1)

In Sylvia Wynter's view (1996: 9–10), 'Columbus's 1492 voyage cannot be detached from' these historic events. The Portuguese tried 'to circumvent the Islamic trans-Saharan monopoly over the rich gold trade' through a sea route, landing first in present-day Senegal. This set in train the drawing of 'parts of West Africa into a mercantile network and trading system, on the basis of the exchange of their goods for gold and slaves and enables a pattern of relations between Christian Europe and non-Christian "idolaters" whose lands were seen as "legitimately expropriable"' (Wynter, 1996: 11). We can mind map how the negative weighting of 'idolater' easily led to the connections, heathen/uncivilized/incapable of governing/lacking intelligence and so on that lay at the base of European cultural and political discourses of/on Black thingification, of Black pathology:

> Cultural and political discourse on Black pathology [...] constitute the background against which all representations of blacks/blackness or (the color) black take place [...] blackness has been associated with a certain sense of decay, even when that decay is invoked in the name of a certain (fetishization of) vitality.
>
> (Moten, 2018: 141)

Indeed, 'Blackness comes into relief against the background of its negation' (Moten, 2018: 242). What Frantz Fanon (2021) calls epidermalization, ensures that Black skin marks and experiences sexual and racial difference through the 'hardening' effect of the racializing gaze (Stephens, 2014).

However, for Michelle Stephens (2014), intersubjective, prediscursive and sensuous knowing take place in the flesh. Thus, there is a tension between Black 'skin' and 'flesh' because racialization fixes skin as flesh. Black skin becomes a sign for racist negation created by a white supremacist discursive order. This discursive order was set in train since at least the Middle Ages, continued into Portuguese exploration of the West African coast, Spanish and other European 'New World' conquest and settler colonialism, Indigenous genocide and dispossession, the Transatlantic Slave Trade and Indenture. Conquest and white settler colonialism functioned on and through the captive African and African diasporic body which was constructed as flesh without humanity, in a context where humanity could only be white European. The captive body, 'this body-with-skin is an organic "resource for metaphor" but also a "defenceless target" for the aims of a racializing discursive order' (Stephens, 2014: 3). In the 'New World' colonies, the captive bodies, first Indigenous then African, were within a symbolic order with new coordinates of gender and race (Stephens, 2014). As such, the only free body was that of the HuMan (Wynter, 2003) read as white European whilst unfree Black flesh 'reveals the markings of the symbolic order on its skin' (Stephens, 2014: 3). Skin matters.

The matter of skin

As said in the previous section, in Kobena Mercer's (1994) view, skin is not just organic matter but the most visible signifier of racial difference. Skin is the largest organ, but it is also a container for who we are and what we can become (Tate, 2009). As Fanon (2021) shows, skin discourses are important in the psychic formation of the colonized as an object of the racializing gaze of the colonizer. This colonizing gaze draws on racialized difference and, indeed, constructs it. Racialized difference lives on in colonial skin scripts that are 'the impositional writings of others on bodies that are not their own [burdening] the body [… regulating] "looking relations", representational gazes, and disciplined surveillance of Black bodies' (Jackson 11, 2006: 3). For Ronald Jackson 11 (2006: 12), such 'scripting is not just about stereotypes and negative images; it is about how the treatment of Black *bodies* as commodities has persisted for hundreds of years and continues today'.

Commodification ensures that 'within the interplay of race relations, corporeal zones such as that of skin color and hair texture automatically evoke feelings, thoughts, perhaps anxieties, if they are already resident or dormant' (Jackson 11, 2006: 10). In other words, skin is a zone of affect and the powerful medium in and through which we live our complex relationships with self and others. 'Skin colour has been the building block of nations, racial affective economies and structural inequality' (Tate, 2015a: 148) within the Western Hemisphere. Skin is also a 'heuristic representing the intersectional meeting point of a Black body subject to symbolic and imaginary capture in racializing discourse and imagery' (Stephens, 2014: 3). The captivity produced by intersectional racialization within Western Hemispheric symbol and imagination relates to Black diaspora communities as a whole. Irrespective of tone, Black skin is intersectional because it is the container of racialized, gendered, sexualized, classed, abled and aged selves, for example. Indeed,

> Dark skin on Black women's [and men's] bodies has become a Black Atlantic diasporic (post)colonial artefact circulating discursively within the skin value hierarchy of racial capitalism [because of] racial capitalism's 'second skin' discourses of dark skin as contemptible object established prior to and during enslavement and colonialism.
>
> (Tate, 2019: 173)

These 'second skin' (Cheng, 2011; Stephens, 2014; Tate, 2009, 2017a) discourses continue within racialized affective regimes which impact Black lives. If one begins from shadism/

colourism and/or whiteness, the impact of 'second skin' discourses can produce alienation from oneself, one's very skin, because of daily shaming events (Tate, 2017a). However, it is also the case that Black women with darker skin dis-alienate from 'second skin' discourses to construct the skins they live in as objects of love rather than shame. They do this by critiquing discourses which reproduce their skins as valueless (Tate, 2019). That is, they engage with a '*heautoscopic* vision – projecting [their] own inside outward as if separate from the self [...] to give it a meaning in the mirror of the gaze that is separate from oneself' (Stephens, 2014: 196–197). Black women's critiques of 'second skin' discourses produce and maintain alter/native constructions of dark skin value (Tate, 2019). This is in itself a radically political Black aesthetic consciousness focused on liberation. These critiques undermine the transgenerational, circumscribed, colonial 'second skin' that continues to condition the politics of hypervisibility (Tate, 2017a) linked to 'the history of normative whiteness, for instance as fear, desire, terror and fantasy' (Tate, 2015b: 186). The fact of Blackness continues to be that Black skin is intensely affective.

Located as an intersectional surfacing marked by and read through inscribed signs, skin takes us to the impact of society and culture on the psyche. This is so because for Didier Anzieu (1990), skin is a key interface between the psyche and the social (cited in Tate, 2009: 57):

> For Freud (1962: 26), the ego has a bodily nature as the 'ego is first and foremost a bodily ego, it is not merely a surface entity, but is itself the projection of a surface'. Didier Anzieu (1990: 63) uses this insight to coin the term skin ego as 'the ego is a projection in the psyche of the surface of the body, namely the skin'. The skin ego encompasses the skin's impact on the mind and 'is at once a sac containing together the pieces of the self, an excitation screen, a surface on which signs are inscribed, and guardian of the intensity of instincts that it localizes in a bodily source, in this or that sensitive zone of the skin'.

Skin impacts the mind and, through the skin ego, it is an excitation screen. Here is where I would also add affects, race and gender to Anzieu's formulation – 'an excitation screen, *an affective racialized surface on which racialized gender signs are (re) inscribed*'. Furthermore, the skin ego (Anzieu, 1990; Prosser, 1998) 'as a sac containing together the pieces of the self', must be thought through race and gender intersections within a 21st century 'post-race' context of anti-Black racism (Tate, 2015b), where racism exists without racists (Bonilla-Silva, 2010), and enslavement, colonialism and coloniality are deniable. 'Skin is material, discursive, psychic, affective, social, political, and skin colour continues to be fundamental to our identities and constructions of the world' (Tate, 2015a: 148). Skin is a site of power and inferiorization. Skin also has material effects as it structures our world and our place within it.

For example, Robert L. Reece's (2020) work asserts that gender and skin tone connect to Black Americans' social outcomes. There is a three-tiered hierarchy of income stratification with light-skinned men at the top with higher incomes, after controlling for other relevant factors, whilst darker-skinned women and men are at the bottom of the hierarchy with lower incomes than medium-skinned men, light-skinned women and medium-skinned women (Reece, 2020). Casey Stockhill and Grace Carson (2021) illustrate that there is gendered colourism in salary recommendations where darker-skinned men were offered less salary than darker-skinned women. In terms of the justice system, Ellis P. Monk (2019) states that dark skin tone is highly correlated to risk of arrest and incarceration in the US. At the level of reproduction, Carol S. Walther (2014) asserts that sperm banks in the US use online catalogues for customers to select sperm donors in which race and skin colour are significant factors. Music is also impacted by skin shade with Wendy Laybourn's (2017) study of Billboard Rap Year End Charts from 2007–2011 showing that lighter skin is significantly correlated to higher chart ratings. Further, Elizabeth Obregon (2020) shows that in some contexts like Cuba which claims to have a 'color blind racial democracy', white ancestry is used in family identity narratives, thereby undermining the nation's racial narration of itself and revealing persistent racial hierarchies. Similarly, in Brazil, racial hierarchies are constantly negotiated in families (Hodge-Freeman, 2013). According to Ginetta Candelario (2007), in the Dominican Republic and its US diaspora, Hispanicity and Indigeneity underlie the national aesthetic preference with Blackness perpetually denied within the '*indio*' ideal. In JeffriAnne Wilder's (2009, 2015), and Stephanie Coard and Alfiee Breland's (2001) research in the US, we see that medium skin tones are preferred to either light or dark skin tones. From the vantage point of the UK, Karis Campion (2019) asks that we think about multiracial (skin) positionings within the Black imagined space because of the 'horizontal hostility' faced by Black 'mixed race' people within Black (thought as non-'mixed race') rejection.

These studies amongst others (Hunter, 2005; Tate, 2015a, 2016, 2017; Telles, 2006; Obregon, 2020), show that colourism has been very much a part of the social landscape of the Western Hemisphere since enslavement and colonialism's light/white skin preference. As the previous examples show, colourism is the basis of inter- and intra-racial discrimination which impacts how we view ourselves and others (Hall, 2017). Colourism also has social effects through long-term, transgenerational accumulation of economic, social and political advantage. The examples alert us to the fact that anti-Blackness takes on nuanced and gendered skin shade forms in the 21st century, but we must remember that these have colonial antecedents as part of the racial structuration of societies. The colonial matter of skin is complex, complicated and continuing.

This book engages with race and gender intersectionality through connecting to affect as it develops Black feminist decolonial analyses of a global anti-Blackness which adheres to skin. As such, it will also add to the subfield of skin studies, that is 'the critical study of the skin' (Lafrance, 2018), as it takes the affects attached to Black skin as its key focus. The book looks at anti-Blackness and racism within institutions (modelling, advertising, films and beauty pageants) and cultural representations, as well as the affects which keep anti-Blackness in play within these fields through reading Black skin affections from a Black feminist decolonial perspective.

Reading Black skin affections

What do I do as a discourse analyst when I read Black skin(s) as text(s)? I think that what I must do in reading is to try and understand how Black skin scripts are 'written, socially interpreted, [that is] how [skin] scripts are disembodied and redistributed within social space' (Jackson 11, 2006: 53). That is, I should try and read Black skin as texts to decipher its meanings within/ across space and time. I must acknowledge that Black skin texts are contingent and contextual, even while I assert that Black skin has been homogenized through racialization. As I have done in this chapter in thinking through the creation of Black skin's construction in terms of racial difference and pathology, I must begin from historical socio-economic and political life. Learning from Black skin's historical positioning in the Black Atlantic diaspora becomes the basis for understanding contemporary accounts/stereotypes/controlling images that underlie 21st-century skin scripts.

As is the case for other intersections, racial and gender scripting, 'refers to the assignment of bodies, as understood by the scripter (for example the media), to certain locations of being, followed by a socio-political values-assessment of those [skins] based on how well they match the scripts imposed on them' (Jackson 11, 2006: 53). It is the 'scripter's autobiographical iterations (projections) left in the final construction' that enables the tracing of the outlines of skin scripts. For example, the white projections of white supremacy and anti-Blackness. These projections can then be strategically deconstructed (Jackson 11, 2006: 53) through reading skin affections. By 'affection' I mean here the process or act of being affected, or of affecting, drawing from the Latin *afficere* 'to influence'. This 'influence' is important because through skin scripts, we can be affected by others as well as affecting others because of affects such as love, hate, disdain, contempt and shame, to name a few:

Affects occur

in impulses, sensations, expectations, daydreams, encounters, and habits of relating, in strategies and their failures,
in forms of persuasion, contagion, and compulsion, in
modes of attention, attachment, and agency, and in pub-
lics and social worlds of all kinds that catch people up in
something that feels like *something*.

(Stewart, 2007: 2)

Affects are ordinary and every day. They are:

public feelings that begin and end in broad circulation,
but they are also the stuff that seemingly intimate lives are
made of. […] They can be funny, perturbing or traumatic
[…] akin to Raymond Williams's structures of feeling,
they are "social experiences in solution" […] Their significance lies in intensities they build and in what thoughts
and feelings they make possible'.

(Stewart, 2007: 2–3)

'Affection is the expression and exchange of affects', where
affects 'are not just perceived as emotion or feelings, but as
intensities, sensations and bodily reactions disturbing, but
also stretching and reaffirming power relations' (Gutiérrez
Rodríguez, 2010: 5–6). Drawing on Teresa Brennan's (2014)
view of affection, we see that we are moved by what touches
us as affects enhance when they are projected outward. Affects
can also be depleted when we carry the affective burden of
another through transfer (Brennan, 2014). Affection exists
within race and gender power relations and affects themselves
emerge within this matrix of domination in 'a concrete historical geo-political context' (Gutiérrez Rodríguez, 2010: 5).
Even as they attempt to escape being named, they emerge in
'the intensities they produce, through the thoughts and feelings
they create' and the 'residues of meaning' they carry (Gutiérrez
Rodríguez, 2010: 5).

Affects are relational. Therefore, in Black feminist decolonial readings of skin affections, I move away from the 'what' of
affect to look at 'how'. As a reader, I become sensitive to the

'manner of the world [...] in the interval between *how* to affect and *how* to be affected' (Seigworth and Gregg, 2010: 15). That is, I attend to the race and gender colonial power matrix and how its residues of affective meaning resonate, and how this resonance speaks anti-Black race and gender narratives which can be *felt, sensed and made into words* and that these narratives have a colonial history.

For example, as I look at an image of the 1632 oil painting by Flemish painter Christiaen van Couwenbergh (1604–1667) (Musée des Beaux-Arts de Strasbourg, Figure 1.1) I feel her despair, fear and anguish clearly demonstrated in the wide eyes, the attempt to flee from the laughing, naked white man holding her pinned to his lap on the bed, the nude white man standing and pointing at the scene with amusement and the fully clothed white man looking on with delight at what is about to happen or has happened already and about to be repeated. Will he perhaps join later in the gang rape? We do not know if this

Figure 1.1 Three young white men and a Black woman, Christiaen van Couwenbergh circa 1632, Niday Picture Library/Alamy.

scene is imagined as taking place on a slave ship in the Middle Passage, a slave fort on the West African coast, a plantation, a settler colony or the metropole. The possible scenes of the gang rape itself make me know that this was/is a possibility for all Black women. *Her fear served as my warning of Black women's vulnerability.* It also made me know that the terror of rape is white men's fun, as we see in the animation on all the men's faces, a scene which we are invited to join by the nude white man who looks out of the painting at us while pointing at her suffering, laughing. The painting displays white men's dominion over Black people in the Dutch colonies and metropole through her body standing in for all Black colonized/enslaved people. *Shock. Anger. Pain.* However, I am mindful that my feeling, sensing and making affects into words only grasps at skin affections fleetingly and always from my Black feminist decolonial standpoint. Grasping at Black skin affection's threads does not aim for universality but is firmly located in Black diasporic spaces, times and experiences.

However, as I feel, sense, read and make skin affections into words, I try not to be reductive of skin's complexities. Instead, I focus on Martiniquan poet, the late Édouard Glissant's (1997) demand for 'the right to opacity'. By this, he insists on 'that which cannot be reduced, [… as] the most perennial guarantee of participation and confluence' (King, 2019: 7–8). Guaranteeing participation and confluence is also about reading into/through/about Black skin freedom from coloniality's anti-Black necropolitics (Mbembe, 2019). A Black feminist decolonial reading strategy, such as I try to engage in the book, foregrounds the making and unmaking of the HuMan, the Black (negro) and the Indigenous (indio) in European empire making (Wynter,1996). These master signifiers emerged in Western Hemispheric histories of genocide, dispossession, settler colonialism, enslavement and indenture beginning with 1441 and the Portuguese introduction of Black Africans to European slave markets (Wynter, 1996). This is the context and space for a conjuncture which produced an anti-Black, anti-Indigenous conception of humanity and construction of Frank Wilderson 111's (2010) and Sylvia

Wynter's (2003) Indigenous-White-Black ordering of the world. I would also like to include People of Colour here. This Indigenous-White-Black-People of Colour ordering which still persists and in the 21st century repeatedly 'requires the death of Indigenous and Black people [and People of Colour] or their transformation into lesser forms of humanity' (King, 2019: 201–21).

For Shona Jackson (2012), European progress and modernity enslaved and converted Black subjects into civilized others but negated and marked Indigenous subjects for death. I would include here that the idea of 'Black subjects as civilized others' was contingent on their acceptance of their own inferiority and white superiority, as Fanon (2021) shows. Further, the Black enslaved were marked for social death (Patterson, 1982) and as property that could be killed with impunity. In the 21st century, white (settler) colonialism resuscitates 'older liberal humanist modes of thought to create new poststructural and postmodern forms of violent humanisms that feed off Indigenous genocide and Black death' (King, 2019: 10):

> Even as Black and Indigenous people and the world bear live witness – on the street, Twitter, Instagram and Facebook – to the real-time murders of their kin and relations, liberal political commentary, the academy and the white left continue to use a form of speech that refuses to name the quotidian spectacle of death as conquest.
>
> (King, 2019: 11)

In the Western Hemisphere, Black people as 'civilized others' were fungible (Hartman, 1997) because of white supremacist domination that marked Blackness in response to the possibility of fugitivity (Hartman, 1997; Wilderson 111, 2010; King, 2019). In Black US Afro-pessimist thought, fugitivity is the struggle for transformation of enslaved 'flesh' into free 'body' (Sexton, 2011, 2018; Hartman, 1997; Sharpe, 2016; Moten, 2018; Wilderson 111, 2020).

If we think fugitivity decolonially through Black Caribbean Hispanophone and Anglophone feminist thought, we must assert the place of maroonage. Maroonage relates to Black agentic movement away from the necropolitical life of colonialism, enslavement and coloniality and towards freedom. Black is expansive and forged extra-territorially in the Black Atlantic diaspora. Diaspora becomes a *movement away from* the land of bondage in thought, imagination, creative expression, epistemologies and critique, rather than *a movement to, an uncritical embedding within*, the land of enslavement. The expanse of the Black Atlantic diaspora is grounded in the traumas of the Middle Passage, a psychological return to Mother Africa as imagined land-psychic space, a turn away from the plantation/fields/ranches, through maroonage as physical and psychic political action. Maroonage as political act was intentional extrication from enslavement, in order to become human and not white property. Black freedom, Black futurity, is not thought of *as or through land* but as extra-territorial relationalities and skin affections across the zones of the Black Atlantic. As I read skin script affections, I also think about Édouard Glissant's (1997) 'errantry' because of both its link to relationalities and its world-making potentialities. This relation is in opposition to totalitarian thought and sees every identity as 'extended through a relationship with the other' (Glissant, 1997: 18). Therefore, I cannot read Black skin scripts without implicating and critiquing white discourses, thought, epistemologies, affects, power and whiteness as a system of domination.

We still have to engage fugitivity/errantry/maroonage in Black feminist decolonial analyses in the 21st century to mark the fact of the Black un-freedom and death caused by rampant anti-Blackness (Sexton, 2011) within the Western Hemisphere. For Robin Kelly (2000), the colonial state has *not* been done away with. We still have colonial states today whose primary difference is the presence of Black politicians, bureaucrats and functionaries whilst colonial economic, cultural and political links with the former colonizers still remain. We cannot read skin scripts without attending to institutionalized and structural anti-Black racism.

'Fugitivity/maroonage/errantry *in* reading' of Black representation in skin scripts, aims to bring the white colonial 'epistemologies of ignorance' linked to white supremacy into view (Mills, 1997, 2007). These epistemologies are significant for Black feminist decolonial readings of Black skin scripts because the 'white delusion of racial superiority insulates itself against refutation. Correspondingly, on the positive epistemic side, the route to black knowledge is the self-conscious recognition of white ignorance (including its black-faced manifestation in black consciousness)' (Mills, 2007: 19). Charles Mills makes clear that the 'white' in 'white ignorance' is not confined to those racialized as white. Indeed, 'providing that the causal route is appropriate, blacks can manifest white ignorance to include moral ignorance […] moral non-knowings [and] incorrect judgements' (Mills, 2007: 22). We must unsuture from white epistemologies of ignorance through a self-conscious recognition of white ignorance as part of generating Black knowledge. We do this by 'reading *into* fugitivity/maroonage/errantry' as a Black feminist decolonial analytical practice. Thus, Black feminist decolonial readings of Black skin scripts become practices of freedom.

When we produce Black feminist decolonial readings, we must also proceed from the understanding that what we will be doing very often is reading against the grain of the theoretical givens. We will be working against the politics that dictates that for Black academics to produce legible work in the academy often means adhering to research methods that are 'drafted into the service of a larger destructive force […] thereby doing violence to our own capacities to read, think and imagine otherwise'. This means that as we read, *we must not* 'reinscribe our own annihilation, reinforcing and reproducing what Sylvia Wynter (1994: 70) has called our "narratively condemned status"' (Sharpe, 2016: 13).

In response to this possible narrative, Christina Sharpe (2016: 12) asks that we become undisciplined in order to produce 'a blackened knowledge, an unconscious method […] of encountering a past that is not past'. In the Western Hemisphere, we remain in the continuing and changing present of enslavement's anti-Blackness and its denial of Black humanity. Anti-Blackness is the Western Hemispheric condition that 'fugitivity/maroonage/errantry *in reading*' and '*reading into* fugitivity/maroonage/errantry' works against and along the grain of. Black feminist decolonial readings elaborate on the skin scripts/scripting of the 'gaze' and 'social prescriptions that disprivilege racialized, politicized and commodified Black bodies' (Jackson 11, 2006: 11).

Book structure

Chapter 2 begins with a brief history of intersectionality, including its present post-intersectionality life, and thinks about the question '*are we really "post" intersectionality?*' as it develops a Black feminist decolonial framing for/of intersectionality. This framing asserts that intersectionality is *intrinsically decolonial*, and we are not yet 'post'. The subsequent chapters look at the intersections of race and gender in Black skin's libidinal economies by thinking through affects – such as fear, anger, fascination, hate, love – and representation. The chapters use readings of skin's hypervisibility/invisibility, consumption and cannibalization in Black women and men in the modelling industry, Black men in grooming advertisements, Black men in films and Black women in beauty pageants to delve into the skin politics of the Global West and its meanings for Black futurity. The conclusion turns to interrogate why skin still continues to matter in an anti-Black world where there is still no guarantee of Black freedom. First, let us begin to feel our way through affect and intersectionality.

2 Feeling our way

Black skin's affective politics and intersectionality

Introduction

As a brown skin Black girl growing up in independent Jamaica in the 1960s and 1970s, my skin gave me something. It connected me to my family's love; my village community's care and it gave me the comfort of familiarity. I read Fanon when I was a teenager, and I didn't really get that my skin was a problem. My Black skin only became a problem when I had a Fanonian moment on arrival in the UK as a migrant in 1975. That is when I really knew what being Black meant as I emerged in relation to the white (wo)man. That is when I understood in a full way what Fanon meant by being a 'Negro' 'existing triply' 'responsible for my body, race, ancestors' because I was 'over-determined from the outside, a slave to my appearance'. That was the first time I was fixed by a white gaze and tongue which asked which part of Africa I came from, where I learned to speak English so well and how I survived Jamaica's ghettoes. This showed the depths of white epistemologies of ignorance/wilful forgetting of white transgenerational benefit from Caribbean Indigenous dispossession, African enslavement and settler colonialism/white supremacy/coloniality/and that class exists in former colonies. Since those early 'welcome but don't come to England days' – as I call them now – of anti-Black hate, much like Fanon, I have had to become a sensor of racism in order to survive and navigate the anti-Black world of the UK. Skin signifies as it 'is inscribed with its own history of serving as a modern sign for

DOI: 10.4324/b23223-2

what it means to be human' (Stephens, 2014: 195). Skin is gendered, sexualized and racialized as '[…] constructions of female beauty and sexuality reflect racial hierarchies of white supremacy and Black subjection' (Hobson, 2018: 10) while, dark 'skin is a masculine sign of potency and has intense psychological implications when contrasted with light skin as a sign of masculine impotency, hence effeminacy' (Hall, 2015: 27).

As my auto-ethnographic account and the quotes show, skin colour, its shade, signifies. It signifies who is human. Skin is also significant for self and others in the interplay of the politics of race, gender, sexuality, class, ability, age, beauty and belonging. Skin is key in the identifications *we construct* and the identities *we are made to occupy* societally. Skin is integral to understanding our lived experiences as intersectional if we think relationally about race, gender, sexuality and class, for example (Collins and Bilge, 2020), through Black skin experiences.

This chapter begins by reading an example of race and gender intersectionality in the HBO television series *Lovecraft Country* before segueing into the problematics of race and gender in relation to the Black body. It then moves to look at the historical development of intersectionality as a theory, concept, methodology and heuristic. In doing this, it will pay attention to the necessity to *not displace* race as has happened within women's studies in the US (Nash, 2018) and women's and gender studies in Europe (Lewis, 2013). Tracing intersectionality's genealogy in Black US feminist thinking and activism, alongside Black feminism in the Caribbean (Reddock, 2007) and Black Latin American/ Hispanophone Caribbean (BLAHC) decolonial feminist thought (Miñoso, 2007 Curiel, 2016), the chapter seeks to establish that intersectionality has always had a decolonizing potential. As such, intersectionality must be a key component in Black feminist decolonial analyses of the affective life of skin colour politics in an anti-Black world.

Race and gender intersectionality on television

I want to begin by sharing some skin scenes from HBO's 2020 supernatural horror series *Lovecraft Country*. This series

is based on Matt Ruff's (2016) book and follows Atticus Freeman (Johnathan Majors), Leticia Lewis (Jurnee Smollett) and
his Uncle George Freeman (Courtney Vance) on their journey
across 1950s Jim Crow US. Uncle George is the author of the
Safe Negro Travel Guide, travelling across the country marking
places that are safe for Black people to visit. *Lovecraft Country*
looks at the real-life horror of anti-Black racism and white privilege in the US. In Episode 5, 'Strange Case' (directed by Cheryl
Dunye), Black, fat Ruby Baptiste (Wunmi Mosaku) transforms
into white, curvy Hillary Davenport (Jamie Neumann) through
drinking a vial of a potion given to her by white, blond, male
love/sex interest, William (Jordan Patrick Smith).

> **Skin scene 1** – After drinking the metamorphosis potion
> given to her by William, Ruby wakes up as Hillary in a
> bedroom in a Black neighbourhood. She is disoriented
> and goes out to the crowded street to Sheffield and Sons
> barber shop in a dressing gown. When a man answers to
> her knock on the window asking if she is lost, Hillary
> says 'I am Ruby Baptiste'. She bumps into a Black boy
> just as two white cops arrive to get her based on her
> husband's call about his missing wife who has fits and
> needs her medication. One cop nearly beats the Black
> boy with his truncheon for possibly molesting Hillary.
> Hillary says that he was only trying to help her, using
> the power of her white skin in that moment to mitigate
> possible anti-Black male violence. The cop replies, 'No
> need to protect this animal ma'am if he did something to
> you'. The people on the street of the Black neighbour-
> hood watch while this is happening without intervening.
> Only her words can stop the police violence against a
> Black innocent. The cops take her home but she begins
> painfully and slowly transforming in the car. The cops
> deliver her home, and William takes her into the house.
> He places her on a sheet of plastic, turns up the television
> so the neighbours will not hear, dons long, yellow rub-
> ber gloves, guts her with a knife and begins peeling off
> her white skin to reveal her Black skin beneath.

Skin scene 2 – While getting dressed after bathing, William speaks to Ruby about metamorphosis. He had been interested in this, but it was only theoretical until he met disgraced academic Hiram Epstein (who experimented on Black subjects, a fact that he leaves out of his commentary), who created the magic through which one could change. Butterflies surround a naked Ruby while he sits on the bed and puts on his socks and shoes. She asks, 'Did I die to turn into that white woman?' William explains that the magic potion only mimics metamorphosis and that it wears off after a while. Ruby then admits that magic scares her, 'It scared the shit out of me to wake up white. Then when I was stumbling down the street, crazed, and dishevelled and screaming at everybody around me, they weren't scared of me. They were scared for me. They all treated me like …' William ends her sentence for her, 'Like a human being. I know your transformation was painful'. Ruby responds that it went beyond pain. She felt that she, 'was being remade'.

Skin scene 3 – She is free to leave William's house but Ruby does not take the money that he has left for her. She only takes the potion and transforms into Hillary. As Hillary, she goes to the white areas of town, the ice cream parlour and the park to read the papers in the sunshine. She then is in the bathtub at William's home as Ruby. William walks in, washes her back and tells her that until the time she does him the favour, she can, 'go wherever she likes, wear whatever skin she likes'. William asks her why she did not take the money that he had left. Ruby replies, 'I enjoyed my entire day using the only currency that I needed…whiteness…. I don't know what is more difficult, being coloured or being a woman. Mostly I am happy to be both but the world keeps interrupting and I am sick of being interrupted'.

Skin scene 4 – Tamara, the only Black employee working in the Marshall Fields and Company department store where Hillary is the deputy manager, is putting shoes on display. Hillary comes over and tells her that what she is doing is wrong. She has to put the white heels with the monochromatic dresses to appeal to their upmarket clientele. Tamara says she does not mean to be disrespectful, but she was doing her best. Hillary retorts, Well your best isn't good enough. You want to be a credit to your race? You have to be better than mediocre and do you wanna know why? Because white folks are even more fucked up than you think they are. They've got shit you can't even imagine. That's why you've got to be exponentially better than them so you don't end up in some closet half dead with your tongue hanging out.

Skin scene 5 – The white members of staff visit a South Side club with Tamara. Hillary's white women colleagues dance with Black men who they have sexually objectified. Hillary's skin begins to shed, and Ruby also peels it off. The store manager Paul Hughes tries to force himself on Tamara in an alley outside the club saying that he could 'smell that she wanted it'. She fights him off. Ruby sees this happening as her white skin falls away.

Skin scene 6 – Hillary tells Paul Hughes that she is going to quit because she is attracted to him. Quitting means that she would not jeopardize his position with the company because of her, 'licentious ways...so quitting is the only option, so I can finally fuck your brains out'. Hillary licks him from neck to chin, stops him from caressing her and controls the domination and submission (D/s) seduction as dominatrix. While she takes off his tie and wraps it around his wrists, she asks him what he wanted to chat about earlier. He mumbles distractedly that he thinks it is time to fire Tamara because she was not pulling her weight. Hillary takes his belt off and wraps it securely around his neck, leading him around like a dog on a leash. With his trousers and underwear around his ankles, he is thoroughly bound. He kneels before her and she tells him to suck the heel of her black stilettoes. He complies. She stuffs a hankie into his mouth, pushes him face down onto the floor and sodomizes him repeatedly and very bloodily with the heel of her stiletto. All this while Hillary's skin begins to fall away. She becomes Ruby as he moans from the pain. She turns him over to face her, putting her stiletto-heeled foot onto his chest. She says, 'I want you to know that a nigger bitch did this to you'. She leaves him sobbing while Hillary's skin continues to peel off.

Skin scene 7 – Ruby asks William what is in the basement because it is the only room in the house that is locked, and only Christina Braithwaite (Abbey Lee Kershaw) and William have the key. William asks Ruby to excuse him, collapses to his knees and has a body transformation of his own. Thin, white, blond Christina Braithwaite emerges from his skin.

All of these scenes speak to the significance of race in the lives of Black and white people in Jim Crow US. They also speak to the entanglement of race and gender in magnifying skin's power, skin's impact and skin's affections within that racial Manichean divide, Black/white. Scene 1 shows the power of a white woman's skin to both demand and receive protection from Black men/people. It also illustrates that protection of white women by the white state through aggressive male police presence and their threat of anti-Black violence in defence of white women is a societal given when white women are held up as sacrosanct. It also shows her ability as a white woman with just a sentence to keep a Black boy who was just trying to help her, safe. However, we also have the complicity of white male police in domestic violence by her white husband, William, as they deliver her to him when she said he treated her badly, and she was afraid. William's act of stripping off Hillary's skin to reveal Ruby is a peeling away of that white woman's privilege to reveal a darker-skinned fat Black woman's body, which in racialized aesthetic hierarchy terms was societally below that of the white woman. This body in fact would historically correlate to the body of the Mammy figure in the US South (Collins, 1990/2022). The white man butchers the white woman to reveal Black Ruby with whom he is sexually intimate. This symbolic death again and again of the white woman, is interesting. In the moment of Ruby's revelation, he also shows that his fetish object is fat, darker-skinned Ruby, the Mammy, constructed as the very antithesis of white beauty. He describes Ruby as being magical in response to her question why he chose her rather than the thousands of other Black women that there are in Chicago. If we locate Ruby as his fetish object, we can see this within the framing provided by the late Black feminist theorist bell hooks (2014: 21) as 'eating the other', having 'a bit of the other'. Here, the US Symbolic Mammy trumps waning white feminine desirability because of white heterosexual desire for transracial intimacy with *her*. Or, since Symbolic Mammy is a construction, it would be better to say with *it* as consumable object. There is then:

> pleasure to be found in the acknowledgement and enjoyment of racial difference. [...] Cultural taboos around sexuality and desire are transgressed and made explicit as the [...] message of difference [is] no longer based on the white supremacist assumption that 'blondes have more fun'. The 'real fun' is to be had by bringing to the surface all those "nasty" unconscious fantasies and longings about contact with the Other embedded in the secret (not so secret) deep structure of white supremacy.
>
> (hooks, 2014: 14–15)

In terms of the foundation of this transracial intimacy, what is significant also here is that Ruby does not allow William to kiss her as Hillary, presenting her cheek instead when he meets her after work. She asks him, 'Do you want to kiss Hillary?' To which William replies, 'I wanna kiss whoever you want me to kiss'. This gives the impression that Ruby is in control of both their relationship and her transformation until he tells her that he now wants her to do him the favour. William says that there is a present in the back of the car with 'her name on it'. Smiling, she opens the box, only to see a maid's uniform. This reduces her back to Symbolic Mammy, complete with the maid's uniform, relegating her to servitude. However, in William's home/bed, she is Symbolic Mammy/magical Black woman with heterosexual power, as his fetish object.

Scene 2 continues the theme of white being the default HuMan, but this time from the perspective of Black humanity in the face of white fear and the possibility of anti-Black police violence. Black people were not scared of her as the white woman Other, but they were scared *for* her, they wanted her to be safe; they treated her like a human being. Ruby shows that 'racist thinking perpetuates the fantasy that the Other who is subjugated, who is subhuman, lacks the ability to comprehend, to understand, to see the working of the powerful' (hooks, 2014: 168). Ruby disrupts the power of the white skin which she occupied by making it visible through being controlled by her Black gaze and her racialized readings of the white world. Her gaze, even when in Hillary's skin, is that of a Black woman. Her Black woman gaze breaks from the 'effective strategy of white supremacist terror and dehumanization during slavery [which] centered around white control of the black gaze [...] To be fully an object then was to lack the capacity to see or recognize reality' (hooks, 2014: 168). As subject, she sees white reality from a Black woman's perspective. Her white skin power disruption brings Black humanness into view.

However, in Scene 3, white female skin power is visible again as she had a wonderful day because the only currency she needed was whiteness. This speaks to the intersectional racial gender power matrix, where although Ruby accepts herself as a Black woman, in reality, she is interrupted in what she wants to do because of the hierarchies of racialized gender. We see some of the dynamics of that interruption in Scene 4 when Hillary tells Tamara that she has to be exponentially better than white people to be a credit to her race and not end up half dead in a closet because white people are 'more fucked up' than she thinks. It is the 'fucked-up-ness' of the white supremacist psyche expressed in symbolic, structural, political and physical violence that interrupts Ruby's life because of her race and gender.

In Scene 5, we see some of this anti-Black woman white supremacist violence manifest in Paul Hughes' attempt to play out plantation intimacies (Sharpe, 2010; Hartman, 1997) with Tamara in an alley. He fully expected her acquiescence to his demands because he is her boss, and like any rapist, he can tell that 'she wants it'. Of course, in his mind, if a Black woman wants it, then it cannot be rape. Black women were always hypersexualized during enslavement, as always willing and wanting it, as a precursor to rape and sexual harassment, and we see this being played out again here. In Scene 6, we could say that watching this scene of Tamara's near rape might have been the catalyst for Hillary's brutality as she is changing into Ruby while sodomizing Hughes with the heel of her stiletto. We also can intimate this because of her anger and her wish that he knows that a 'nigger bitch' did that to him. Certainly, that is how he would have been viewing Tamara in the alley because her skin would have spoken 'nigger bitch' to him. Ruby as self-proclaimed 'nigger bitch' unseats white male heterosexual, middle-class supremacy in that moment of brutalization and pain. A moment in which the pleasure of D/s becomes the pain of total domination by someone societally beneath him because of skin. White maleness is also undone when Christina emerges from William's skin in Scene 7. William is only skin because he was killed when he was shot in the back by the captain and dumped in the river. She is the reality that drives that fiction of white male supremacy. We also see the fiction of white male supremacy in a peculiar scene witnessed by Ruby when, as a member of the serving staff in the uniform provided by William, she is hiding in a closet at the club where men talk business as 'The Brotherhood'. She places a stone object in the captain's desk as requested by Christina and then has to hide in a closet so that she is not discovered. She hides in the closet with a white man bleeding from his mouth who is being tortured by Captain Lancaster and his cronies to reveal the location of 'the loot'. Lancaster asks for a new shirt and begins to unbutton his, revealing a Black man's torso as he changes. He is clearly one of Hiram's experiments encapsulating the best of both racial worlds in a white supremacist view. The Black man's brawn and vitality hidden under the civilizational cloak of clothing, topped by the white man's brain and visible white skin/facial features. White male supremacy needs Black male dissected body parts to maintain its privilege and power whether assimilated as part of the white body, or as Billy Holiday's 'strange fruit' hanging from a lynching tree. Hortense Spillers (2003) already made this case in terms of Black women. That is, that whiteness as a structure of domination and white women need Black women in order to come into being through the principle of opposition. This colonial principle of racial and gender opposition is based on troubled categories historically.

Race and gender trouble: the Black body

Race and gender as they relate to the Black body are historically troubled categories. Indeed, according to Tommy Curry (2017: 50):

> To the European ethnologies that served as the basis of the nineteenth-century account of race, gender simply did not exist *within* the Negro race. Blacks were primitive and as such had not yet evolved to the level of civilization necessary to warrant distinctions between men and women. As purely sensual beings, they had no reflective sensibilities that could grasp the purpose of gender roles, which was to ground civilization, much less the morality of femininity or burdens of masculinity according to nineteenth century racial sciences.

Black people 'had not yet evolved to the level of civilization necessary to warrant' gender distinctions, whilst the continent of Africa itself was constructed as feminine in the nineteenth century (McClintock, 1995). Africans did not have genders, but 'in relation to the white race the Negro race was feminine' even though after puberty *'feminine'* Black men were 'predisposed to rape' (Curry, 2017: 53–54).

Oyèrónké Oyewúmì (1997) fleshes out the intricacies of the African gender question further through looking at the emergence of the gender binary in Yorùbáland as a construction of colonialism, the history of which was written from a male point of view. Women were peripheral, if they appeared at all. Colonialism was cis-gendered, hetero-sexualized, and male colonizers used European gender understandings to determine policy. That is, they implanted European gender bio-logics which constructed 'native' (that is, African) women as the unspecified category 'Other' with the category 'native' read as male (Oyewúmì, 1997). The colonial race–gender order meant that white women were above both colonized women and men. Further, British direct rule did not acknowledge the existence of female chiefs who were stripped of power, with recognition as leaders only being given to men. This meant that women were effectively shut out of colonial state structures and land ownership based on sex/gender as a colonial patriarchal imposition. As well as this, Christianization introduced the white European invention of women into Indigenous African religious systems (Oyewúmì, 1997). Oyewúmì's (1997) work shows us that gender is a historico–socio–cultural category conceived in different but overlapping ways in the metropole and the colony (Vergès, 2021).

Another problematic is that the white constructed category black as a signifier of negation is itself a historico–socio–cultural category. Kwesi Tsri (2016) explores the emergence and development of the description of Africans as black. He asserts that Ancient Greeks were the first to think of African peoples in colour terms through Homer's *aithiops*, that is, 'Ethiopian' which meant 'burnt-faced'. This was later applied to African continental people south of the Sahara Desert. However, the term black had a long negative use predating its use for Africans (Tsri, 2016). In Rome, the word *ater* equated to blackness without lustre which resulted from burning and had negative connotations. The term *niger* was shiny, glistening, the colour of night, death and evil, while *furiae* a colour resulting from mixing red and brown, was also attributed like *ater* and *niger* to the skin of those labelled 'negros' (Tsri, 2016). Tsri calls this Greco-Roman origin as well as early Christianity the stage of proto-racism when attitudes and semantic-conceptual systems categorized Africans as black. The Middle Ages and Early Modern English (for example, Shakespeare's *Othello*) were also important historical periods for the emergence and reinforcement of black as a signifier of anti-Africannness/

Blackness which still exists today (Tsri, 2016) impacting Black men, women and children.

'Racist misandry' (Curry, 2017: 106), the hate of Black males and their economic, political and sexual dehumanization is based on this history and is central to 21st-century anti-Blackness. This current century's anti-Blackness like others before it 'animate policy, police-state violence, and white vigilantism [which] desire [...] the death of Black men. [...] Currently, Black maleness is conceptually confined by its social result – Black Death – rather, than life, sociality' (Curry, 2017: 111). The persistence of Black death and Black male death is behind the disregard for and disgust towards Black male life (Curry, 2017). I would also add here that the persistence of Black woman death is behind the disregard for Black women's lives, and the persistence of Black trans death is behind the disregard for Black trans lives.

According to Tommy Curry (2017: 20), 'Staples's *Black Masculinity: The Black Male's Role in American Society*' [... already spoke of a] dual dilemma [...which] sounds like contemporary theories such as intersectionality in that it suggests that every subject is raced and sexed'. This idea was published in 1978 a decade before intersectionality was developed (Curry, 2017). However, it most likely drew from Black feminist thinking on interlocking oppressions/the simultaneity of oppressions available at the time Combahee River Collective (1977; Bell et al., 1982). Jennifer Nash (2018), in *Black Feminism Reimagined: After Intersectionality*, charts the history of the institutionalization of intersectionality in the US academy within women's studies programmes that then has created a Black feminist defensive attachment to its 'knowledge as property'. She insists instead that we should see the intimate entanglement between Black feminism's 'intersectionality' and transnational feminism's 'decolonization' as we let go of the desire to make property of knowledge. According to Nash (2018: 69), intersectionality has travelled far from its Black feminist activist intellectual roots to be institutionalized by feminism as an analytic which can describe everyone's 'identities, experiences and locations'. This accounts for its success as an analytic within the academy transnationally as it 'helped to erode the episte-mological boundaries between those who "know" and those who "experience" by suggesting that experience could be the ground of theory making' (Lewis, 2013).

In *Innocent Subjects: Feminism and Whiteness*, Terese Johnson (2020) argues that despite Black critique of imperialist and racist feminism, racism exists within contemporary British feminism because whiteness is re-centred. This re-centring occurs despite increased scholarly and activist attention to intersectionality and difference. The re-centring of whiteness occurs because white feminists maintain innocence of racism and white supremacy. Johnson's book critiques white feminist appropriation of inter-sectionality whilst claiming to be innocent of racism, and in fact, such appropriation makes their claim to being antiracist possible while white feminist supremacy continues. Françoise Vergès (2021) makes a similar point in her decolonial critique of feminism in France and what she calls 'civilizational femi-nism'. That is, a white bourgeois feminism that through the ideology of equal rights has contributed to continuing domi-nation based on class, race and gender because such feminism spans neoliberal, nationalist-xenophobic, extreme right-wing, capitalist, extractivist and fascist politics.

Critiques and adoption of intersectionality abound. For example, Patricia Hill Collins's (2019) *Intersectionality as Crit-ical Theory* uses intersectionality to theorize social inequalities so as to enable change. She argues that intersectionality could be a critical social theory that could be used to reshape the world, but its assumptions, epistemologies and methodologies must be looked at. Tommy Curry (2017: 37) provides insight into one of its shortcomings when he asserts that theories like intersectionality have no 'explanation for the grotesque – for the disproportionate death and dying of the Black male, the display of his corpse'. Patricia Hill Collins and Sirma Bilge (2020) analyze the emergence, growth and outlines of intersec-tionality in an introduction to the field to show the diversity of its applicability and its potential for looking at inequality as a precursor for social justice change. We also see this potential in Caribbean decolonial feminist thought.

Black Latin American/Hispanophone Caribbean (BLAHC) decolonial feminist thought (Curiel, 2016; Espinosa Miñoso, 2019) draws on intersectionality in its critique of white feminist and colonial reason and the need to develop alter/native thought and practice. Afro-Dominican decolonial feminist Yuderkys Espinosa Miñoso (2007, 2019) speaks about the need to 'develop a genealogy of experience' because of the coloniality of a Eurocentric feminist reason that remains permanently hidden behind the veil of the need for women's engagement with feminist struggle. This is also relevant for hegemonic spaces which have pretensions of universality. Espinosa Miñoso writes out of what she calls regions of the world where modernity is revealed as racist, androcentric, capitalist, imperialist, colonialist, where hegemonic southern feminism is committed to hegemonic northern feminism and coloniality. This continues the history of colonization and dependency producing *la otra de la otra* (the other of the other). She proposes that we decolonize feminism using critiques produced by anti-/decolonial theories from Black women, women of colour and Indigenous women that show that Western modernity was an imperialist, racist project of death and domination.

Afro-Dominican feminist Ochy Curiel (2016) shows the theoretical contributions made by Afro-descendant Latin American and Caribbean women to decolonial thought within the dominance of the nation state, political dependencies within capitalism, European colonization and modernity and the racialization and sexualization of social relations. For her, it is important to remember that the world system of coloniality today is not just centred on Europe but also on the USA, which also establishes hierarchical power systems at economic, cultural, social and symbolic levels. Black women's/Afro women's movements in BLAHC from the 1970s mobilized around race, sex, culture and sexual orientation amongst other identities, locating themselves outside of 'modernity as they identify themselves as not white, heterosexual, nor from privileged class positions and, even, not women' (Curiel, 2016: 48). This genealogy of thought and activism connects to US Black feminism and women's subordination at the intersections of sex, gender, class, race and sexuality. In decolonizing the category woman, Black/Afro Latin American and Hispanophone Caribbean decolonial feminists have stressed the importance of experience and exposed the intersection of systems of domination of race, class and sexuality. Curiel (2016: 50) stresses that in order to continue the decolonial project within a context produced by capitalism and Western modernity, we must understand decolonization as:

> […] the recognition of the economic, political and cultural historical domination resulting from European colonization of other peoples and the effects produced by coloniality in our social imaginary. Decolonization is a political and epistemological position which traverses individual and collective thought and action; our imaginaries, our bodies, our sexualities, and our ways of being and doing in the world. This necessitates a kind of 'cimarronage' from imposed and colonized social practices and the construction of 'other' thoughts in accordance with our lived experience.

Curiel (2016) suggests that strategic essentialism is important for Black/Afro political movements, but Black or Afro must intersect with other oppressions and histories of resistance and transformation. She invokes *cimarronage*-maroonage (Goldson, 2020; Greg, 2016; Walcott, 2018) as significant in this resistance and transformation. I have already described this in the introduction as Glissant's (1997) errantry, or Afro-pessimism's fugitivity, and included this in my Black feminist decolonial *readings of and into* fugitivity/maroonage/errantry as decolonial agentic political action. Curiel also insists that counter-hegemonic projects are necessary against neoliberalism, the neocolonial state and multinational corporations which perpetuate structural racism. This is important to note because capital is consubstantial with the colony (Vergès, 2021), and racial capitalism (Robinson 2019, 2021) continues unabated. BLAHC feminist decolonial thinking aligns closely with the removal of the barrier between theory and practice because the production of theory is a social practice, and there is no social movement without political discourses. Further, class and its intersection with racism and sexism must be re-conceptualized to enable collective action. The Afro/Black feminist movement must also establish political alliances, for example with Indigenous communities, in opposition to neoliberal globalization and extractivism. What is important to note here is that these BLAHC feminists have a clear view that does not confuse colonization as an event or period with coloniality. Coloniality is the continuation of social formations resulting from colonialism where contemporary intersections of racism/sexism/heteronormativity/trans-/homo-phobia/classism/ableism/ageism pervade domination even when colonization has ceased (Vergès, 2021).

In the Anglophone Caribbean, feminist scholarship from its inception has been committed to intersectional analysis. For Patricia Mohammed (2002: xx):

> gender scholarship in the Caribbean has never limited itself to an examination of gender identity. There has been a constant scrutiny and cross-examination of gender with the categories of race, ethnicity, class, age and regional difference by scholars of the region.

Rhoda Reddock (2007a) supports Mohammed's view on intersectionality when she looks at how Caribbean feminists addressed ethnic, class and racial differences. Reddock (2022) identifies what she calls an 'indigenous Caribbean feminism', drawing on Mohammed's earlier work. That is to say, Caribbean feminism emerged from the racialized and colonial gender histories of Caribbean peoples and is located within anti-colonial struggles. Reddock (2022) traces the emergence of Caribbean feminist movements through the work of the Right Excellent Marcus Garvey's United Negro Improvement Association (UNIA) and Pan-African feminists such as Amy Ashwood Garvey and Amy Jacques Garvey, Una Marson and Audrey Jeffers. For example, Jamaican journalist, Amy Jacques Garvey writing in the official publication of the UNIA the

Negro World 'Women as leaders nationally and racially' (October 24, 1925: 5), positioned Black women at the forefront of anti-colonial struggle in the interwar years (Goldthree and Duncan, 2018). Jacques Garvey said, '[T]he doll baby type of woman is a thing of the past and woman is forging ahead prepared for all emergencies and ready to answer any call, even if it be to face the canons on the battlefield'. Jacques Garvey was central in Black Nationalist and antiracist movements in the interwar years. In the Anglophone Caribbean, nationalist anti-colonial struggles opened avenues for women's organizing, contributing to the growth of early feminist movements (Reddock, 2022). Pan-Africanist activism by early Caribbean middle-class and working-class feminists was embedded within their concern for the social uplift of their 'race', colonized 'nation' and class. Many of the women activists of this period called themselves 'feminists', and both detractors and supporters used it as a description of these women and their socio-political work and interventions. In the interwar years, these Pan-Africanist women were anti-colonial and feminist advocates for Black and Indian Caribbean women's rights, especially poor and working-class urban and rural women.

Indo-Caribbean feminisms emerged at the same time in the 1980s as second wave Caribbean feminism, and both are inextricably intertwined because of 'the openness of Caribbean feminist thought and its multiple epistemological and political traditions' (Hosein and Outar, 2016: 4). Gabrielle Hosein and Lisa Outar (2016) trace the genealogy of Indo-Caribbean feminism through indenture and post-indenture experience rather than through an Indian subcontinent diaspora framing. This connects to global sites of Indian indenture such as South Africa and Mauritius, and considers the transoceanic, bringing into view the subject making and remaking journey across the *kala pani* (dark water) to the Caribbean. Indo-Caribbean feminism was developed specifically within the interstices of post-enslavement, post-indenture societies, so it is embedded within 'cross ethnic solidarities and relationalities [because of the] necessary flexibility, inclusiveness, intersectionality, relationality and solidarity of Indo-Caribbean feminist thinking'

(Hosein and Outar, 2016: 15–16). Indo-Caribbean feminist thought advanced theorizing on the intersections of Indianness, Caribbeanness, gender and feminism to change gendered, political and sexual knowledge economies and inequities within the Anglophone Caribbean (Hosein and Outar, 2016). Caribbean feminists reject the division of the world wrought by colonialism, enslavement and indenture between Wynter's (2003) HuMans with the right to life and freedom, and those subalterns of the plantations, slave ships and *kala pani* destined to die.

Conceived as theory, methodology, heuristic and concept, intersectionality has been generative within Black/Afro/Third World feminist thinking in the Global South and North, even as Eurocentric feminism disavows and displaces the critical race theory, and Black feminist intersectional antiracist activism and intellectual endeavour from which it sprang (Lewis, 2013). From these roots/routes, intersectionality has been rethought and revised, including by 'post-intersectionality' scholars who developed new terms such as 'multi-dimensionality', 'assemblage' and 'hybrid intersectionality' to enable a connection to affect (Nash, 218). Of course, I would argue that intersectionality already connected to affect because its subject was the Black woman of 'love politics' (Nash, 2020). However, unlike Jennifer Nash, I would say that this radical feminist politics did not challenge intersectionality but was an active part of it and also enabled complex analyses of the operation of anti-Black woman hate. As Nash (2020: 440) herself says

> [June] Jordan was not the first to put love at the centre of her Black feminist project; a few years earlier, the Combahee River Collective Statement noted that its proto-intersectional politics "evolves from a healthy love for ourselves, our sisters, and our community which allows us to continue our struggle and work" [...and] Black feminist love politics remains a political and rhetorical trope even in contemporary Black feminist scholarship.

Placing Black feminist love politics within the Combahee River Collective Statement also extends the Black feminist project to include sexuality and class as did Audre Lorde's (1984 and 2007a) and Angela Davis's (1983) seminal texts.

Affect is central to the theoretical and activist work of Black feminist decolonial analysis and intersectionality, specifically so as it relates to the experience of the normalizing power to constrain and the potential to create the world outside of the horizons of the racialized gender contract (Pateman and Mills, 2007) which we currently inhabit. Racialized gender injustice and Black deaths lead to affect (grief, anger, despair, fear, hate, love, for example) being viscerally felt as intensities which pass body to body. As these resonances circulate, they build political community through their erotic life (Lorde, 2007a) as they stick to bodies and worlds (Ahmed, 2014; Seigworth and Gregg, 2010). Indeed, affect:

> at its most anthropomorphic is the name we give to those forces – visceral forces beneath, alongside, or generally *other than* conscious knowing, vital forces insisting beyond emotion – that can serve to drive us toward movement, toward thought and extension, that can likewise suspend us (as if in neutral) across a barely registering accretion of force-relations, or that can leave us overwhelmed by the world's apparent intractability.
>
> (Seigworth and Gregg, 2010: 1)

However, affect need not be 'especially forceful', it can also be subtle, unnoticed, 'a gradient of bodily capacity [...] that rises and falls [through] encounter [and] sensation and sensibility' (Seigworth and Gregg, 2010: 2). Affect is intimate but impersonal, relational but distant in its body-body passage as it marks skin's racialized gender belonging/unbelonging to the world that it encounters. A world where 'Black cannot reach the plane of being' (Wilderson 111, 2010: 38). Using the Spinozian formula of 'to affect and be affected', Brian Massumi (2015) asserts that affect is proto-political. I would say that affection is political with a potential to provide decolonial impetus as it includes relationality, an openness to encounters in the world in which one is affected by and one affects others. 'Affect is a dimension of life-including of writing, including of reading-which directly carries a political valence' (Massumi, 2015: vii). Western Hemispheric racialized gender skin politics cannot be thought, read, written or be the focus of liberation movements without affection. It bears repeating that skin has an affective life. What more can we then say about intersectionality and skin politics from a Black feminist decolonial perspective?

Intersectionality and Black feminist decolonial skin politics

On the subject of intersectionality, its intellectual creator, Kimberlé Crenshaw (1989, 1991), asks us to think in combination. As we think in combination, we should pay attention to how race, class, gender, sexuality, ability and age, to name a few intersectional categories, produce new social positionings. When we think intersectionally, we should think of new social positionings rather than seeing intersectionality as an adding together of categories. Drawing on Crenshaw, for our purposes here, we can say there is a difference between darkskinnedwoman, a new social positioning and, woman and dark-skinned, which adds categories together. This difference is not only one of academic argument. It is a difference that speaks to race and gender skin affections and their (dis) attachments in the case of darkskinnedwoman and to skin as a scene of positive affective evaluation and affirmative politics. In the case of woman and dark-skinned, what we see in this adding together is skin as a site of negation within social processes such as class and generational wealth, and intimate relationships.

For Jared Sexton (2018), within an anti-Black world, Black women and girls have it worse than Black men because of their social locations, for example, the intersections of race, gender and sexuality which augment racialized gender inequity under capitalism. As such, they do not share equal oppression with Black men and boys (Pateman and Mills, 2007; Sexton, 2018), and are not exempt from continuing to die at police hands as we see from Breonna Taylor (USA) in 2020. According to Sexton (2018: 90), in the US, Black people inhabit a 'scenario where [our] murder is required for others' peace of mind [... which] hold together the very basis of the [anti-Black] status quo, shoring up the cracks in its foundation, bolstering the platform of its reproduction'. We can see this in the development of both #SayHerName and #BlackLivesMatter. On April 20, 2021, 46-year-old George Floyd's murderer, white former Minneapolis police officer Derek Chauvin who had knelt on Floyd's neck for 9 minutes and 29 seconds ignoring his pleas that he could not breathe, was found guilty on all counts – second- and third-degree murder and manslaughter – and, sentenced to life imprisonment. Three other officers present at the scene of Floyd's murder faced trial in 2022, accused of aiding and abetting murder and manslaughter and violating his civil rights. On February 24, 2022, Tou Thao (is Hmong American and kept bystanders back), J. Alexander Kueng (is Black and knelt on Floyd's back) and Thomas Lane (is white and held Floyd's legs) were each sentenced to 25 years in prison for violating Floyd's civil rights in depriving him of his right to medical care. Thao and Kueng were also charged with failing to intervene to stop Chauvin (the *Guardian* 'Three Ex-Officers Found Guilty on Federal Charges in George Floyd Killing' Associated Press, Thursday February 24, 2022, accessed 2/24/2022). These killers being brought to justice was thanks to the undeniable truth of a video shot on a phone by Darnella Frazier, who was on her way to the convenience store with her 9-year-old cousin on May 25, 2020. This video of Black male death spurred the #BLM global movement in 2020. After her video went viral, this traumatized teenage girl was harassed on social media. She should not have borne witness, and she should not have let others do the same. She should have been silent. Her witnessing ensured a crack in the reproduction and silencing of anti-Black racism.

All over the Western Hemisphere where black as white stereotype emerged as negation, needing to be contained and killable, we see the texturing of class, gender, sexuality, ability and age by race intersections as Black women, men and children continue to occupy zones of coloniality. In these zones of coloniality, Black feminists struggled to produce theory that explained, reflected and supported their lives as lived. The centring of Black women's lives as lived rather than as the black of white stereotype; the refusal of the splitting of oppression so that Blackness was also inextricably about sexuality, gender, class, ability, age, for example; the bringing to the fore of Black women's contributions including to Black activism; and the critique of white power and epistemic privilege are significant for locating intersectionality's decolonizing potential and force.

Further, Black male studies scholars' (cf Curry, 2017; Kitossa, 2021) critique of and drawing on intersectionality shows that *the black man* is not ahistorical but colonially constructed, as predator, rapist, criminal, violator. Black maleness is also about dehumanization, making Black men and boys vulnerable to physical, emotional, sexual and psychic violence, denial of the possibility of being a theory-producing subject, and living within the possibility of death in an anti-Black world where they are thought to be disadvantaged solely based on their race. Black men and boys were consumed sexually, through cannibalism and labour extraction during colonialism and enslavement (Aldrich, 2002; Curry, 2017; Hyam, 1991; Kitossa, 2021; Woodard, 2014).

To claim as I do that intersectionality has always had a decolonizing potential is not just to relate this to the impact of Third World feminism's anti-colonialism/imperialism on US Black feminism (Nash, 2018) through its calls for decolonization as central to self, collective and state transformation (Alexander and Mohanty, 1997). It is also to say that intersectionality developed over centuries of activism and theorizing within a Western Hemispheric post-enslavement white settler colonial space which meant that decolonization was already implicated in its emergence. The very choice to centre Black women as the bodies, intellects and souls from and about who theorizing and activism would begin was already a decolonial act and continues to be so.

I want to draw again from Vergès (2021) here to pull together the threads of Black feminist decolonial thought based on thinking that intersectionality *has always been* decolonial. For Vergès (2021), when we say decolonial, we actively remove feminism from its white, European, bourgeois life and affirm our alliance to the struggles of women of the Global South who came before. Decolonial feminism is anti-capitalist, anti-racist, de-patriarchalizing and anti-imperialist, as said above citing Espinosa Miñoso's work. Women in the Global South have entered a new stage in decolonial thinking and activism as they denounce rape, femicide, militarization, dictatorships, dispossession, coloniality, extractivism and death (Vergès, 2021). Like Black feminist intersectionality, decolonial feminism rejects the reduction of Black women's struggles to integration into the neoliberal equality order and refuses 'civilizational feminist' complicity with racial capitalism (Vergès, 2021). Decolonial feminism rejects misogyny/misogynoir, homo/trans-phobia, anti-Blackness, anti-Indigenous racism, cis-heteropatriarchy, ableism and classism, in its demand for equity. Its demand is for equity between knowledge systems allied with its contestation on the canon of Western epistemologies in its re-visioning of the construction of the world by white supremacy. In this re-visioning, decolonial feminism contests the making of Black/Indigenous/Asian/African peoples into subalterns incapable of reason, technical and scientific discovery, and in aesthetic terms, 'ugly'. It also rejects carceral and punitive regimes, extra-judicial killings, Indigenous dispossession and continuing extractivism (Vergès, 2021). Decolonial feminism is at base about struggles against whiteness as a structure of supremacy which still animates 21st-century coloniality and underlies the violence meted out to people racialized as other. I will then bracket the (post) in post-intersectionality critiques to show that we are not yet past the necessity for intersectionality. This asserts the necessity to maintain intersectional thinking within Black feminist decolonial theorizing and activism in a context where we still actively engage coloniality as part of lived experience within the continuing struggle for intersectional racial justice and social justice transformation. That is, intersectional thinking is still necessary in a context of Black un-freedom in order to add nuance to social justice critiques and demands as we see in #SayHerName. Intersectionality means that skin must be thought through a Black feminist decolonial lens.

Thinking skin through a Black feminist decolonial lens

We have seen in the introduction and in this chapter the importance of skin politics as it relates to the possibility of decolonial feminist politics in lived Black intersectional experience. I now want to move to a body of Black feminist work which would not claim the space of decolonial critique but which I place within that perspective. I place this work here as I have said elsewhere (Tate, 2020a) because of its active turning away from Eurocentricity, its disalienation (Césaire, 2000) from its epistemic violence, to an envisioning of Black feminist epistemological and ontological futures. To this end, the late Nobel Laureate Toni Morrison (1994: 8) points us to the way forward in terms of African-American scholarship which we can apply to a decolonization of Western Hemispheric and global knowledge systems. We can see what decolonization means when she speaks about the dangers of totalizing approaches and dominance. We should bear her warning in mind as we feel, think and write our way towards other futures:

> I do not want to encourage those totalizing approaches to African-American scholarship which have no drive other than the exchange of dominations-dominant Eurocentric scholarship *replaced* by dominant Afrocentric scholarship. *More interesting is what makes intellectual domination possible; how knowledge is transformed from invasion and conquest to revelation and choice; what ignites and informs the literary imagination and what forces help establish the parameters of criticism.*
>
> (my italics)

Morrison states the challenge for Black feminist decolonial critique. That is, that as we oppose coloniality, including its epistemic violence, we should not fall prey to its long-standing focus on erasure and total replacement to maintain dominance. As we oppose coloniality, we should not have to repeat its doxa or the episteme of only this or that knowledge being worthy of inclusion in building the disciplinary canon. We have to move away from knowledge as conquest and hegemony towards what Morrison calls revelation and choice. By revelation and choice here, I am taking her to mean the need to struggle for equity between knowledges and contestation about what counts as knowledge as we revise the Eurocentric narrativization of the world in which racial capitalism (Robinson, 2019, 2021) transformed people from Africa, Asia, the Caribbean and the Americas into inferior commodities incapable of reason, technical and scientific advances and devoid of beauty. We have to see ourselves as doing more than being opposed to, however, if we are to build something new, to build towards Black feminist decolonial futures.

We have to take up Morison's and Édouard Glissant's (1997) challenge of life beyond mere 'opposition to' and construct something new through critique. Black feminist decolonial critique challenges othering, highlights continuing coloniality and turns away from white settler supremacist domination. What Morrison shows us in this turning away view is that knowledge linked to invasion, dispossession and dehumanizing trauma is necessary in Black feminist decolonial critique to ignite knowledge, personal commitment and political transformation. For Vergès (2021), we must engage transnationally with decolonial feminist struggles from the Global South but also remember that decolonization and decoloniality can also be co-opted by capital and put to use in its name. We see that, for example, in a proliferation of decolonization as a word in European universities and the European Left in which it is completely shorn of its focus on racism. We also see that in the pervasive insistence in UK, US, French and German 2020–2021 'culture wars' that colonialism no longer matters as they are now 'post-race', or at least, multicultural societies. In other parts of the Global North such as Scandinavia, race and anti-Black racism are still erased, and the place of their colonial and enslavement pasts in their formation as wealthy nations remains silenced.

As I write and think through writing, I still keep circling around and coming back to Wynter's (2003; 2001) assertion that being HuMan was a verb *not* a noun. Therefore, humanness was curtailed for Black communities as part of the European genres of the non-HuMan during colonialism and enslavement. This produced an alienation from the self and community as Fanon (2021) showed us in his critique of the Black colonial psyche. A Black feminist decolonial critique including self-critique actively seeks out and acts against coloniality's alienation. It does this through disalienation (Césaire, 2000), the active, consciously enacted, turning away necessary to bring Black people and People of Colour into view as humans, and refuse white dominant intersectional racialization discourses, representations and imaginaries that we have all inherited, even when we do not want them. Turning away through refusal can be intellectual, psychological, political, but it can also be viscerally felt and can lead to community building through affection. Refusal is not new and underlies what Curiel (2016), noted earlier, calls 'cimarronage', 'maroonage' (Goldson, 2020; Greg, 2016; Walcott, 2018); Glissant calls errantry; and which I have called fugitivity/maroonage/errantry in reading and reading into fugitivity/maroonage/errantry.

The late Caribbean American feminist Audre Lorde (2007a) speaks about the necessity of refusal through theorizing the erotic as an inner resource, a power vested in our (un)recognized feeling. Lorde insists that we must recognize our deepest feelings to refuse suffering, self-negation and numbness and to act against intersectional oppression. For her, affect is politically important because Black feminist intersectional communities can be built through joy. Trinidad and Tobago feminist M. Jacqui Alexander (2006) builds on Lorde's work by looking at 'erotic autonomy' in Black feminist praxis as a decolonial project. Like Lorde, Alexander sees decolonial feminism working from a need to break down false boundaries between theory and practice. Breaking down boundaries means that theory articulates with activism so that voice can be given to that which has been unspeakable. This refusal of unspeakability, of silencing, is necessary for the liberation of self and community. Refusal enables Black feminist decolonial critique to restore dignity and make the world intelligible.

Conclusion

What would it mean to decolonize Black skin as a status, an imaginary, a negative affective force? In other words, if 'aesthesis[1] is connected to decoloniality, how do we emancipate our very senses from the standards of beauty formed through the colonization of our very eyes, ears and tongues?' (Ortega and Lugones, 2020: 274). In response to this question from Mariana Ortega, the late decolonial feminist María Lugones states that in 'decolonial aesthesis', there is a decolonial deconstruction of aesthetics that privileges the senses. Here, Lugones meditates on how to do away with gender by thinking about 'the coloniality of embodied female aesthetics' within the racialized female body crossing from coloniality's 'female animals' to decoloniality's 'being a self' (Ortega and Lugones, 2020: 276). Part of coloniality's animalization was located on the very skin of racialized women, men and children to which were attached negative affects such as fear, hate, contempt and fascination. Therefore, I would also like to add here the question: 'How can we emancipate racialized skin's affects from the negation of colonization?' That is, to use Gail Lewis's (2013) words, how can we look at the 'subterranean affective flow' of Black skin to enable its decolonization?

The cultural analyses of representations in this book will do some of this work through a Black feminist decolonial perspective on (post-) intersectionality which does two things. First, it argues as we saw in this chapter, that because of its origins in Black feminist activism and critique of whiteness and Eurocentrism, intersectionality has always had a Black feminist decolonizing impetus from its very inception. Second, the book aims to feel its way through the subterranean affective flow 'which buries itself within or rests on the skin of an utterly corporeal body' (Brennan, 2014: 3) that exists at the intersections of race and gender. The next chapter turns to modelling, racialized fascination and skin shade.

Note

1 Aesthesis is an unelaborated elementary awareness of stimulation, the process of perception.

3 Racialized fascination

Modelling and skin shade[1]

Introduction

Models are part of a global aesthetic labour force which moves from show to show and fashion week to fashion week right across the world. Their body parts – faces, lips, hands, legs, feet, teeth, bottoms, skin – adorn advertisements and, although small in numbers, their bodies occupy catwalks from Milan to London, to Paris, to Tokyo, to New York, to Sao Paolo, to Seoul, to the Caribbean. In 2015, British model, Jourdan Dunn spoke out against an industry in which racism was still rife, much as Naomi Campbell and Iman did before her. Racism was so institutionalized in fact that lighter-skinned Dunn claimed that there had not been a Black model on the cover of British *Vogue* since Naomi Campbell decades previously. In June 2020, Beverly Johnson, the first Woman of Colour to appear on the cover of American *Vogue*, said the 'fashion industry pirates blackness for profit…while excluding black people and preventing them from monitizing their talents. Managing racism is one of the things the fashion industry does well'.[2] The world of fashion in which we are led to believe that you make it because you have 'the look' is still rife with institutional racism even whilst we get the exceptions such as Campbell, Iman, Kai Newman, Dunn, Alek Wek and 'Queen of the Dark' Nyakim Gatwech, who are Black models recognizable in Euro-America and beyond. If the modelling industry is ruled by 'the look', then how did these women break through its anti-Black woman skin colour

DOI: 10.4324/b23223-3

politics in which light/white skin is still iconic? Johnson's notion of 'pirating Blackness for profit' gives a way into the chapter's discussion of 'the look' of racialized fascination.

The analysis seeks to decolonize fashion in terms of racialized skin aesthetics and affects within a racialized present by first looking at fashions and racisms before moving to 'the look' and the racialization of modelling as global aesthetic labour in which bodies are negatively racialized through difference, cannibalized and consumed. This is conceptualized as occurring through 'the look' of racial dissection (Fanon, 2021; Yancy, 2008), in a context in which fascination continues to carry colonial misogynoir (Bailey and Trudy, 2018) and anti-Blackness because darker skin is still negatively valued by the colonial gaze. We must remember here that the colonial gaze of racial dissection is not just relevant for those racialized as white but for everyone who is a signatory to the racial contract (Mills, 1997). The chapter then segues to fashion as a racialized present through considering the scene of the emergence of the Black male body in urban fashion as an antidote to its previous relative absence in haute couture. Let's move to looking at fashions and racisms.

Fashions and racisms

Although referred to as 'capitalism's favourite child' (Sombart, 1902: 316 quoted in Briggs, 2013), fashion has a long history, and its origins in ancient China (Hua, 2011), India (Mohapatra, 1992), Egypt, Mesopotamia and Persia (Houston, 2012) have been the subject of detailed inquiry. The theory of global racialisation newly defined as polyracism by Ian Law (2014) also confirms the necessity of identifying and examining racism's complex multiple roots, for example in ancient China and in the Mediterranean region, and the variety of contexts and modernities in which it has subsequently developed. Fashion and racism are long-established phenomena found in many varieties of pre-modern contexts, yet predominant theory in both fashion theory and racism studies tends to equate them with the advent of Western capitalist modernity.

A global theory that strives to be adequately explanatory while not claiming universality needs, therefore, to go beyond these restrictive Eurocentric accounts and give due weight to the operation of these two socio-political processes – fashion and racism – outside the West (Craik, 1993; Law, 2010). Having said that, this book's focus is the Western Hemisphere which highlights its weakness in this regard.

Notwithstanding this shortcoming, it is the case that the conceptualization of the relationship between fashions and racisms remains poorly understood. Fashion has been defined as 'an unplanned process of recurrent change against a backdrop of order' (Aspers and Godart, 2013: 171), and to expand this, 'a way of doing and making things that is bounded by space and time'. Here key aspects of fashion's conceptualization also include fashion as diffusion, imitation by a social set, demarcation and distinction from others and disintegration with the absorption of fashion into mass activity (Simmel, 1957). Georg Simmel (1957) shows that we simultaneously desire to distinguish ourselves from each other as we desire to imitate others. Simmel's work on fashion is also marked out by its uncritical and colonial use of the idea of race. For example, he compares the dress of 'primitive races' and their lack of fashion to that of 14th-century Venetian nobles also lacking in fashion, as they were all obliged by law to wear black. Fashion is also conceptualized as not being exclusively restricted to studies of clothing and dress but it could be applied to many fields where aesthetics operate in conjunction with the processes of fashions and racisms. For example, an article in *Fashion Theory* by Robin Kelley (1997) on the changing meanings of the Afro examined the political contexts in which this hair fashion became popular, and the meaning that Black activists, hairstylists and ordinary Black people gave the Afro. Kelly sought to re-write the history of Black hair, illustrating one of the many other contexts that can fruitfully be explored.

As sign of Black consciousness, liberation and insurrection with roots in the Black Power Movement, the Afro remains highly politicized when it is attached to Black African descent skin. This stylization necessitates kink for volume and height

(Tate, 2017b). Its volume and height, if we take Angela Davis and American civil rights activist and former quarterback for the San Francisco 49ers Colin Kaepernick as an older and a 21st-century example, are linked to assumptions about radicalism. The Afro still resonates with its Black Power past, but there has also been a 21st-century resurgence of the Afro which does not signify Black radicalism *per se*. The depoliticized Afro is a hairstyle that speaks 1970s 'retro-cool' as well as becoming part of Black traditional styling to show Black consciousness and pride. Indeed, to quote Angela Davis (1994: 38), the Afro 'has survived disconnected from the historical context in which it arose' and from the 1990s has become part of contexts that nostalgically privileged it as 'fashion-revolutionary glamor'. Further, as a 'pastiche…the imitation of a particular style…a neutral practice' it has lost its critical or political edge (Davis, 1994: 42). The Afro's co-optation by capitalism's markets in urban Black style has undoubtedly robbed it of its Black Nationalist radicalism (Tate, 2017a). As we see from this discussion on fashion, there are some gaps in our understanding, including comparative studies of fashions of the same 'idea, object or representation' in different contexts, as we see from the Afro. Further, we need to undertake systematic examinations of the interconnections between fashions and racisms.

The conceptualization and theorization of racism have been much too extensively addressed to enumerate the field here. However, racism is defined here as comprising two core elements in all historical and geographical situations. First, it presupposes that some concept of race is being mobilized and, second, it involves negative attributions being made to a specified racial group. Identifying when and how race is being utilized and represented and how negative attribution is being articulated in particular situations are the two central problems that social scientists have faced in establishing the existence of racism across the globe (Law, 2010). Racism is not assumed to be everywhere nor is fashion. This, therefore, requires sharp specification of exactly when and where these social forces are at work. For example, Georg Simmel (1957: 541) speculates that fashion 'does not exist in tribal and classless societies'.

This is a very particular definition of fashion based on ideas of consumption, production, markets, design and the construction of taste through brands and branding. Aspers and Godart's (2013) definition suffers from conceptual inflation in seeking to broaden and deepen the meaning, significance and reach of fashion as a concept to the level that it becomes vague and generalized. As such, it fails to provide the analytical tools to answer the questions of exactly what and what does not constitute fashion. This is a problem that has also dogged the conceptualization of institutional racism, including in the fashion industry. In this definition 'process', 'change' and 'order' could refer to many different types of phenomena, for example, how do we differentiate fashion from war, as both could be described as processes of change against a backdrop of order? We could only revert to the aesthetic, the construction of taste and the governmentality of the cultural/economic/social/political 'capitals' (Bourdieu, 2021) of fashion as a racialized industry.

Aspers and Godart's (2013) over-generalized position derives from Herbert Blumer's (1969) assertion that the domain of fashion could apply to any sphere of human activity operating through 'collective selection' where fashions are created and then subject to distinction and imitation across and within social groups rather than simply the 'reverential' imitation of the upper classes. Specifying fashion conditions, as with the notion of racial conditions, can be used to sharpen theorization. For example, human 'choice' – although constrained through Foucauldian (1995) biopolitics and racial capitalism's markets, for example – is a pre-requisite of fashion as is the notion of a specified aesthetic or prevailing judgement of taste. Let us see if we can change the geography of reason on fashion, by turning away from these more Eurocentric logics and looking at theorizing fashion focused on the Global South.

Looking South at fashion and style

In interrogating postfeminist aesthetics, Simedele Dosekun (2020: 26) looks at what she calls 'spectacular femininities' in Lagos, Nigeria. Through that prism, she sees fashion as, the changing styles of clothing, beauty and adornment as a practice and mark of distinction, desire, and creative self-making [which] is among the things that some would deny African women, imaginatively, conceptually but sometimes also physically, even violently. So too is feminism.

The fact is that in Africa as is the case elsewhere, fashion and beauty are political, structural, shaped by power and constitute affective ties to who we are and who we cannot/should not be (Dosekun, 2016). Dosekun (2020: 27) points out, that 'fashion and self-fashioning are African traditions' in order to

refuse at once notions that fashion is unique and endogenous to Western capitalist modernity counterposed to the 'dress' or 'costume' or 'garb' – implying the 'exotic', 'essential', 'premodern' – of the non-West. Indeed, even 'traditional dress' is invented with textiles and other goods from internal and external locations having a part in its fabrication. Further, new approaches to styling, design, tastes and values impact 'traditional dress' [which is] fluid, syncretic and contingent.

(Dosekun, 2020: 27)

African continental fashion is part of flows of materials, designs and tastes historically through trade across the African Continent, the Atlantic and Indian Oceans and through the religions of Islam and Christianity (Dosekun, 2020). We can use cloth as an example of this flow within colonialism, globalization and racial capitalism. African prints were developed by European companies, for example in Manchester, UK, in the 19th century using batik from Java and sold to West African markets. This cloth now signifies Africanness, specifically West Africanness, but it is also shaped by local tastes and desires in garment design. For Dosekun (2020: 27–28), 'African print' is performative, as it is about 'the invention and authentication of Africa and the assertion of African nationalisms on and through the dressed body'. 'African dress' enacts both 'anti-colonial resistance and post-colonial nation building [because] modern European dress codes

[were] central to the self-declared civilizing missions of colonialism and Christianity in Africa' (Dosekun, 2020: 28). Traditional dress exists alongside a variety of other ways to dress and look fabulous for women in Lagos, Nigeria (Dosekun, 2020). This shows that there is no essential Africanness held within fashion as this is constructed through self-fashioning and stylization including with 'Western dress'. Western dress has been available since the 1600s as ready-made clothing sold by European companies (Dosekun, 2020). Through the routes of markets and colonialism, Western dress established itself as the normative 'modern standard', a 'global dress' which has also been incorporated into African fashion and stylization over many centuries (Dosekun, 2020: 29). Thus, spectacularly feminine women in Lagos look exactly like African women keeping in touch with global fashion across the Black Atlantic's sartorial, makeup, hair, taste and stylization flows, with Rihanna and Beyoncé, for example, being part of a transnational 'Black look' (Dosekun, 2020).

We all seek beautification as humans, irrespective of race and gender. Michael McMillan (2017) illustrates this search for beautification but also the local impacts of transnational Black male style in his analysis of Black men's diasporic agentic sartorial stylization in the UK from 'saga bwoys' (1950s drawing on US 'zoot suits'), to 'rude bwoys' (1960s drawing on Jamaican gangster style) and 'saggers' (1990s onwards drawing on US urban styling). We can also see this if we turn to look at dancehall men (Figure 3.1) in Jamaica and *Sapeurs/Sapeueses* in Kinshasa (Democratic Republic of Congo) and Brazzaville (Republic of Congo).

Donna Hope (2010) examines what she calls one of the most controversial expressions of Jamaican masculinity in dancehall culture, 'Fashion Ova Style' aesthetics. This stylization reconfigures masculinity to include feminized aesthetics, public presentation of the male body in dance performance and high levels of male homosociality in the public performance space' (Hope, 2010: 124). In this refashioning, the 'hard bad man' can wear pink and tight trousers, for example, as part of male transgressive fashioning rituals. 'Fashion Ova Style reflects the cross-fertilization with high fashion and style

Figure 3.1 Dancehall star Elephant Man, Everynight images/Alamy.

from the developed capitalist metropoles, American hip hop culture, and the historical imperatives for African flamboyance and ostentatious costumes. (Hope, 2010: 124)

Hard-core dancehall men prefer high fashion even within the traditional restrictions on Jamaican masculine styling. They also engage in facials, manicures, pedicures, eyebrow shaping and hair styling, which were once seen as taboo because they were feminized and feminizing practices. Dancehall men now have intricate cornrows and other hairstyles, plucked and fashioned eyebrows and lightened skin without their masculinity or heterosexuality being brought into question by their audiences. The well-cared-for body is then adorned with expensive, imported, global brand name clothes (Moschino, Versace, D&G); gold, diamond and platinum jewellery; and shoes like Clarks from the UK. This 'bodily care [...] purportedly signals wealth, luxury and high status' (Hope, 2010: 126). As these trends make clear, there is constant cross-fertilization with global/local codes of fashion and style in dancehall culture. For Hope (2009: 126), the Fashion Ova Style dancehall men produce a 'gangsterized, hardcore and feminized masculinity that is highly transgressive and revolutionary'. Fashion Ova Style masculine aesthetics also includes tattoos, hair colouring and colourful costumes.

La Sape, Société des Ambianceurs et des Personnes Élégantes (Society of Ambiance Makers and Elegant People; Figure 3.2) is a fashion subculture in low-income communities in Kinshasa and Brazzaville. A *La Sape* follower is called a *Sapeur* (man) or *Sapeuse* (woman) or *minisapes* (children) (Schreiber, 2021; Zaidi, 2020). Since the 1920s, *Sapeur/euse* have been making fashion statements on the streets through designer clothing and stylization which challenge societal power dynamics and, in the case of *Sapeuse*, hetero-patriarchal norms. Style remains necessary in spite of the grinding poverty in the Democratic Republic of Congo and the Republic of Congo, and perhaps because of it. However, even as whiteness is upended in these examples, whiteness is not the ideal everywhere; in other words, Black bodies remain trapped within racial capitalism.

Figure 3.2 Society of Ambiance Makers and Elegant People: *La Sape*, Frederic REGLAN/Alamy.

Whiteness is not the ideal everywhere: Black bodies in racial capitalism

In the contemporary world universal, Eurocentric beauty ideals of thinness, whiteness and Anglo-American features have been much criticized for the globalized domination of Western beauty imperialism in fashion contexts. However, this perspective tends to deny human agency in the construction of racialized and gendered bodies. For example, Angela McCracken's (2014) ethnographic study of Mexican young people's beauty ideals and practices shows this, as does the previous example of the race performative (Tate, 2005) power of the Afro. Tate (2009, 2010), Dosekun (2020), Hope (2010), Cooper (2010) and *La Sape* also show that whiteness is not the global ideal, as, indeed, does the 'Ebe' chosen as the most handsome man in the Bonara-Aboure people's Popo Carnival in the Ivory Coast. The Ebe's beauty emanates from his vigour, deeds in society and his bravery. In 2022, Ettia Kouassi Paul was elected (Reuters, 2022; Figure 3.3).

Figure 3.3 Ettia Kouassi Paul, elected as the 'Ebe', the most handsome man, waves as he takes part in a parade during the Popo Carnival, Reuters/Alamy.

A survey of articles in *Fashion Theory* illustrates the useful, but uneven and unsystematic examination of global processes of racism and fashion. Carol Tulloch (1998) has also argued against a Eurocentric account of the study of dress in her work examining the dress practice of African-Jamaican, White-Jamaican and Indian-Jamaican women from various social strata of Jamaica between 1880 and 1907. Tulloch unpacks the multiplicity of meanings associated with colonial dress. In exploring fashion and racial aesthetics in contemporary Jamaica, Carolyn Cooper (2010) challenges the privileging of racial hybridity as the symbolic marker of national identity, setting nationalist rhetoric against populist, African majority constructions of Jamaican identity. She evaluates the significance of Caribbean Fashion Week in challenging globalized, racialized fashion aesthetics through its showcasing of a high percentage of Black male and female models wearing spectacular designer clothes which she uses to illustrate a 'permissive modelling aesthetic' that enables multiple readings of the body as cultural text (Figure 3.4). Further, the development of a modelling industry in Jamaica

Figure 3.4 Female models painted for a promotion for Taboo before a show at Caribbean Fashion Week at the Sports Arena in Kingston, Jamaica, Robert Landau/Alamy.

that 'valorizes idiosyncratic style' is identified as opening up a central role for Black-originated and focused images of beauty.

Janice Cheddie (2010) also examines contestations of racialized fashion in her work on the conceptualization of the urban street as a site of racial and political authenticity for the Black subject and the associated linkages between this and formations of race, resistance and concepts of Black style. She examines Tom Wolfe's essay 'Radical Chic' (1989[1970]), the media image of the Black Panthers, and fashion images from *Harper's Bazaar* (UK) 1968–9 and shows how fashion commentary, fashion theory, documentary photography and social protest impacted upon the visualization of the Black body within 1960s fashion photography and subsequently. The privileging of a masculine subject in these texts is also subject to critical interrogation.

This theme is further examined in Sarah Gilligan's (2012) work which looks at the 'fragmentation of the Black male body' through representations of clothing and desire and the case of Will Smith. Dorinne Kondo's (1997, 2003) work also seeks to contest Western racialization and explore counter-Orientalisms in her examination of Japanese high fashion and Asian American theatre which are used to interrogate the politics of pleasure, the performance of racial identities, and the possibility of political intervention in commodity capitalism through contesting representations of Asia. These critical debates provide a powerful set of conceptual and analytical tools and substantive evidence to develop a global sociology of fashion and racism but there are many gaps here, not least the omission of major geo-political regions and, for example, the patterns of production and race and gender performativity involved in the plethora of Fashion Weeks across the world.

Racism in the fashion industry in the UK was exposed by Annie Phizacklea's (1990) study of the West Midlands area in the UK, focusing particularly on production. The specific racialization of modelling has also been the subject of regular critique (Mears, 2011). This has prospered through a conspiracy of silence amongst agents, models and photographers with little emerging onto news media agendas. In the 1990s, a high-profile voice that challenged this institutional silence was that of Naomi Campbell, whose critical comments were reported in depth in April 1997, in 'Prejudiced Fashion Bosses Insult Me as the Black Bardot' (The Sun April 11, 1997). This story was covered in both the tabloids and the broadsheets and provided easy and appealing linkages to be made between celebrity, 'race' and the female body. An 'anti-racist show' of sympathetic coverage of these comments from the press was not enough to constitute a serious challenge to the industry. These comments could be easily dismissed as 'the un-substantiated carping of the tantrum-prone rich and famous' (Gary Younge, 'The Trends That Make Beauty Skin Deep, *Guardian* November 24, 1999). The BBC programme *Macintyre Undercover* provided incontrovertible evidence that racism in the fashion industry was endemic, and further evidence from footage not used in the programme was reported in the *Guardian* ('Race Bias Attack on Top Model Agency, November 24, 1999). Hostile references to Black models as 'niggers', systemic misogynoir and systematic exclusion from modelling opportunities, for example in Milan, were shown as prevalent features of the world's largest modelling agency, Elite, and in particular the views of its top executives. This provides some explanation for the lack of response to Naomi Campbell's earlier criticisms, as this is the agency that represented her. The exclusion of Black models from the covers of fashion magazines, and in particular the removal of Naomi Campbell from the cover of American *Vogue*, which prompted her comments, is seen as common business sense as the 'sales drop by 20%' when Black models are included, as a spokesman for Jean Paul Gaultier once said (Gary Younge, *Guardian* November 24, 1999). Inclusion or exclusion of Black models relates to the profit margin making judgements at the time of who to include on covers or have on the catwalk, not neutral but racist.

Over ten years later, the *Guardian's* Hannah Pool acknowledged that '[f]ashion probably is a bit racist' (*Guardian* February 22, 2011). She reported the comments of the Carole White Premier Model Management, '[I]t is a lot harder to start a black girl than a white girl, photographers and makeup artists are scared, everyone is scared, if I take that risk will she sell my products? It's driven by what sells and in general white blond girls sell'. As model booker Anne Wilshaw said, '[I]n Milan black girls never work, in Paris it's still the same'. Hadley Freeman's article 'Why Black Models Are Rarely in Fashion' (*Guardian* February 18, 2014) provided further journalistic support for this critique. Recently, Van Beirendonck , a Belgian designer used 'Stop Racism' placards on his models as a critique of the misuse of Native American headdresses on the catwalk (Lisa Charleyboy Runaway Antiracism Message: Headdress No More' CBC January 18, 2014). Tyson Beckford, a Black US male model also confirmed that 'racism is due to the decisions of designers, stylists, bookers and agencies' (*Esquire* interview January 17, 2014, 'Tyson Beckford on Modelling, Zoolander and Racism in the Fashion Industry'). He stated, '[F]ashion is one of the most racial industries out there now'. In New York, the Fashion Week absence and patchy presence of models of colour was regularly charted by *Jezebel. com*, and comments from Black models including Beverley Johnson, Chanel, Iman, Joan Smalls and Jordan Dunn have all confirmed the many and varying forms of racial discrimination, racially exclusionary practices and racist discourse in fashion contexts. Anais Mali confirmed the 'tales of racism in the fashion industry [range] from ridiculously insensitive editorials to the whitewashing of runways' (Julee Wilson 'Another Black Model, Anais Mali, Shares Her Tale of Blatant Racism in Fashion Industry', Huffington Post February 3, 2014).

One reaction to the uses and abuses of Black and People of Colour women's and men's bodies in global racial capitalism has been the commodification and 'consecrating' of race-specific beauty evident in Black *Vogue* (2008) and Oriental *Vogue* (2011), analyzed by Giselinde Kuipers et al. (2014). They show that the promotion of racially diverse standards of beauty is contested so long as it remains 'glamorous' and 'fabulous'. Glamourous and fabulous are prerequisites, but even these are not race neutral categories, as what this racial segregation in *Vogue* demonstrates is that as well as being about capturing market share in different global locations and racialized constituencies, whiteness is prevalent, 'the look' is racialized in modelling, and determines who can participate in modelling as global aesthetic labour. That is, whose body, skin, is aesthetically valuable and will produce profits because of its cross-over capacity globally.

'The look', modelling and global aesthetic labour

Models are part of a global aesthetic labour force which moves from show to show and fashion week to fashion week across the world.

However, if we decipher 'the look' which they are supposed to have as being to do with beauty, we already see that it is not neutral. The gaze at 'the look' which determines its beauty comes from a specific location (Tate, 2009). That location is one in which there is a continuing racialization of beauty in societies in which Black skin and hair continue to matter within their existing racial structuration and racial evaluations of human worth (Banks, 2000; Carroll, 2002; Craig, 2022; Gilman, 1985; Hobson, 2005; Tate, 2005, 2007, 2009, 2017a, 2017b). Notwithstanding negative evaluations, Black women's, men's and children's body parts-including skin- can be and have been commodified. Not only is there a racializing of beauty in which white/light skin is still the ideal, but there is a use of the body of Black women, men and children as models which keeps that norm in place in Euro-America. This use is related to establishing racialized difference through skin, hair, facial features and representation, which serves to set Black models apart, whether they are supermodels or not. Thus, what we have on catwalks and in ads is an anatomical economy of beauty and the look as *outsideness, exoticism and difference* in a context in which beauty as visible, as inscribed on the body's surface, *matters*.

The matter of racialized difference is an interesting one in terms of the look because it is not necessarily about being 'the most beautiful', however that is defined, but being unusual enough to sell. Again, we go back to the global market in Black skins and the profit motive. For example, Alek Wek's difference from the norm of 'the look' was so great that the

Figure 3.5 Sudanese top model Alek Wek pictured during the Yves
          Saint Laurent presentation of fall/winter fashion in Paris,
          July 11, 2001. dpa Picture Alliance/Alamy.

late Karl Lagerfeld declared the blond to be dead (Tate, 2009;
Figure 3.5). This did not mean, of course, that whiteness
ceased to have a place in modelling but that it had been *decentred* by a new look. 'The look' has *value* in terms of selling Black
women's bodies while designers of *haute couture* like Lagerfeld
sell cloth and design. The look also maintains aesthetic value
or instantiates new approaches to the global aesthetic labour of
model bodies in terms of the visible markers of race.

What this makes us recall is that 'beauty' – the look – is
constantly re-negotiated, re-fashioned and re-inscribed on the
surface of the body, on its skin in other words, because skin
continues to be the most visible marker of race, as said previously. 'The look' within modelling is a very potent piece of
'wisdom' and a 'rule of conduct' (Foucault, 1995) whose power
has emerged through long histories of repetition within the

industry, but the parameters of which remain unclear to out-siders. 'The look' renders invisible the racialization of beauty and its impact on the lives, psyches and bodies of Black models (Craig, 2022; Gilman, 1985, 1992; Hobson, 2005; Rooks, 2000; Russell et al., 1992; Tate, 2007, 2009; Taylor, 2000). We just have to look at the past media storm about Naomi Campbell's traction alopecia from years of wearing very tight weaves to comply with the straight hair rule of super model status to see the impact of 'the look'. Hair can be seen as *much more than just hair* within a context of the racialization of beauty in modelling where the only beauty 'truth' is 'the straight hair rule' (Taylor, 2000). Hair is merely organic matter but carries profound racialized meaning in terms of beauty (Banks, 2000; Craig, 2022; Mercer, 1994; Tate, 2005, 2017b; Taylor, 2000). This is linked to the fact that 'within racism's bipolar codifi-cation of human worth, black people's hair has been histori-cally *devalued* as the most visible stigmata of blackness, second only to skin' (Mercer, 1994: 101). As a norm, 'the straight hair rule' of 'the look' is not necessarily explicit but remains implicit within the psyches and practices of sociality. As a result of its normalization and the fact that straight hair is taken for granted across a range of racialized groups, this norm is therefore diffi-cult to read as a beauty norm. We can only discern the norm in the effects it produces (Butler, 2004).

However, we can say that beauty cannot, or does not, come from within; it is socially constructed and performa-tive (Tate, 2009). Therefore, skin/body/face/ hair defined as Black within the Western Hemisphere through the *appearance* of Blackness has been constructed as being outside of the realm of 'the beautiful' because of racialization. So what is the beauty that 'the look' seeks out and produces on the Black woman's body? What is it that is of value as a Black model? What is of value is the visible racial difference that is *certain*. What is of value is also delineating 'the look' in different *perceived* racial types, including that of 'mixed race' women. Alongside keep-ing racial typologies alive within our 21st-century psyches, the look also produces bodies for sale on the global catwalk so that worldwide women can see bodies which can extend to theirs through racial branding (Wingard, 2017). The use of racial branding as a marketing tool also means that modelling establishes itself as a meritocratic global workplace, one just has to be tall, thin, young, and have 'the look' in order to be chosen by modelling agencies and get launched on an international career. Or, so the story goes.

Within the racialized anatomical economy that is modelling, how can Black women break through? They can only do that as the exception, and this exceptionality has changed from the 20th to the 21st centuries. Naomi Campbell, for example, had to continue to exemplify Black women's animality, which we saw decades earlier in Jamaican Grace Jones. Jourdan Dunn now has to produce Black, middle-/upper-class chic which is transracially recognizable, much like Michelle Obama had to in order to become the first African American FLOTUS (Tate, 2012). When Dunn speaks, she 'keeps it real' as a Black British woman, but on the catwalk and in her public life, she cannot reproduce 'ghetto fabulous' or 'Black glamazon/diva' through her clothes, makeup or comportment. Being an exception is not very exceptional, as there are rules of conduct which maintain exceptionality because 'the look' of racialized skin fascination from the location of whiteness produces what it desires to see, what it always already knows about this or that zone of its construction, *the black woman's* skin.

The look of racialized skin fascination, consumption and misogynoir

The bold statement has been made in the previous section that modelling is institutionally racist, but what does this mean for Black models as global aesthetic labourers whose bodies, skins, lips, noses and hair are sites of fascination? As aesthetic labourers, their bodies produce economic, political, social and cultural capital for the design houses and the women who then go on to buy 'the look' extended to cloth or accessories. When that extension to the body of the consumer is accomplished, the Black model's body ceases to have value, as its job is complete. Extension to the consumer's body occurs through affective attachment emerging as a desire to look like that in that particular attire, if only momentarily. Desire for the other, the feeling of wanting or needing to have something is the first phase of avid consumption, 'eating the other' (hooks, 2014) which for Frank B. Wilderson 111 (2010) is part of the libidinal economy of racism.

There is an afterlife to the aesthetic and cultural value of the Black woman's body though for those Black women who identify with these models as beautiful, as role models, as who they aspire to be like. We see this for example in actor Lupita Nyong'o's (*12 Years a Slave; Black Panther*) revelation that until she saw Alek Wek, she did not think of herself as at all beautiful because of her dark skin. Nyakim Gatwech and Nyong'o show that darker skin on a Black woman's body still speaks aesthetic marginalization and that racism is a part of modelling just as fashion is a racialized present (Tate, 2019).

Sheena Gardner and Matthew Hughey (2017) found from a content analysis of mainstream Black and multiracial market-focused magazine articles that the 'tragic mulatto' trope was still dominant, as it was consistently drawn on, resisted and reproduced in magazines in the mid-20th to early 21st centuries. This shows a paradoxical position in terms of the presence of anti-Black stereotypes even within multiracial representations. What Gatwich, Nyong'o and the continuation of the 'tragic mulatto' trope in modelling illustrate is that fascination with racialized skin and its consumption are linked to misogynoir in the 21st century. Anti-Black woman racism abounds even within the 'acceptance with provisos' of 'exceptions'. They are reproduced in the Global Northwest as exceptions because they are the antithesis of the ideal as we see in Lagerfeld's declaration that the blond was dead. What is consumed through the bodies of Black models is racial difference, what bell hooks (2014) describes as a 'bit of the other'. Consumption is enabled through fascination (Tate, 2015a) and, as Stuart Hall (1997) asserts, the act of looking can have a sexual, erotic aspect to it. This suggests that looking involves an unacknowledged search for an illicit desire which can also be unfulfillable. Fascination connotes obsession, spectacle, wonder, but also hate, disgust and contempt (Tate, 2015a). Consumption makes racial other-ing complete, as it is done from the space of a universal white structural domination which is made invisible through 'the look' of Blackness produced from whiteness itself. The look of white dissection in modelling is also gendered in terms of what skin colour is desired on Black women and men as we see if we look at Black male skins.

Devaluation of darker skin on women's bodies but not men's: Black male bodies, the urban and fashion as a racialized present

Black men have been relatively silent compared to Black women on how skin tone affects them (Potts and Johnson, 2020). Kimberley Jade Norwood's (2014) transdisciplinary edited collection examines colourism's emergence from colo-nialism and enslavement in the US, showing its distinction from racism and examining its unremarked but influential ubiquity that affects us all irrespective of gender. In opposi-tion to Norwood, I would say that colourism in the Global North and South-West is a symptom of enduring, persistent anti-Black racism. This impacts Black women and men dif-ferently. For example, Ronald Hall (2015: 27) states that dark 'skin is a masculine sign of potency and has intense psycholog-ical implications when contrasted with light skin as a sign of masculine impotency and hence, effeminacy. [...] Black males are the psychological icons of Western masculinity'. There is a catch to this, however, as we see if we look at the dark-skinned Black male body in enslavement which underlies their iconic status in Western masculinity.

According to Tommy Curry (2021), analyses of Black men found in history, feminist thought and popular culture are dom-inated by narratives and caricatures of lack, hypermasculinity or sexism. Curry warns that we should pay attention to how the necropolitics (Mbembe, 2019) of Black male death plays into and supports anti-Black racism. Anti-Black male narra-tives and caricatures are a part of Black male necropolitical and biopolitical life because they produce a 'distancing negativity'

(Curry, 2021). Indeed, for Curry (2017), anti-Black male racism is a form of misandric aggression reproduced as lethal violence through murders, incarceration, police killings and economic isolation. Coloniality and white supremacy maintain misandric aggression or sex-specific targeting of Black males. What Hall (2015) calls the icons of Western masculinity are under threat, and that makes us wonder what continues their iconicity other than the white lie of their hypermasculinity.

Tamari Kitossa (2021) undertakes what he calls a 'depth analysis' of Black men in art and representation. In his view, the work of propagating erotic tropes and representations of the other occurs through language, representation and symbology. That is, through the operation of culture and its particular structure of feeling (Williams, 1977) on Black male skin. In Western art and cinema, Black men's representations reify the hegemonic notion that they are hypersexual, priapic (that is, relating to or resembling a phallus) and are rapists. Drawing on the work of James Baldwin and Frantz Fanon, Kitossa asserts that this three-pronged trope – hypersexual, priapic, rapist, that is, the 'Black Phallic Fantastic' – is a part of the psychosexual building blocks of Western cultures. In these cultures, there is a continuous recycling of sexual mythologies about Black men through art, photography and cinema which span the centuries. Erotic sexual racism is based on the formation of anti-Black male psychologies and frameworks of practice in which cultural media play a large part (Kitossa, 2021). The white supremacist construction, circulation and recycling of sexualized representations of Black men is the ontogenic basis for Black men's ritual degradation and destruction as forces which threaten civility. The breaking apart of Black men's bodies occurs through a simultaneous fear of and desire for Black men because they are persistently naked in the popular white imaginary even while clothed. This white fear/desire construction haunts white individual and collective ontology (Kitossa, 2021; Curry, 2021).

White fascination with Black males as phallus has a pre-Atlantic slavery existence since Ancient Greece and Rome and continues today within the Western Hemisphere. In the 5th and 6th centuries BCE, Athenian art began to represent satyrs in plays and effigies as 'ithyphallic Africans' (Kitossa, 2021). In Greek mythology, satyrs are beasts with the head and torso of a man and the hoofed body and genitalia of a horse (Kitossa, 2021). For Ancient Greeks, the erect penis of the satyr was a sign of bestiality, not manliness, and although Romans seemed to be enamoured with large penises, this did not mean respect for African men, who were seen as barbarians and subjected to disparaging humour (Kitossa, 2021).

Early Christian iconography and theology carried this sexualized moral geography about African men which became in the West, the Black-man-as-penis. This stereotype carried the assumption that the darker the skin, the larger the penis. For example, the art of Robert Mapplethorpe reproduced and normalized the Black penis myth, so we can see 'the Black man' emerging as an artefact of white supremacist cultural constructions. Black men continue to be fetishized as they are fixed in the desire-fear gaze of white dissection of their genitals. This pornographic one-way scopophilia (Freud, 2016) in itself can constitute erotic satisfaction as the sexualized Black male spectacle enables affects like disgust, contempt, revulsion and fascination (Kitossa, 2021). What is important about one-way scopophilia is that one is not looked at, or perhaps it is better to say that if the look is returned it is not given any attention, any importance and can be erased. As Kitossa (2021) reminds us, the Latin *fascinum* means both phallus and magical spirit, and the Greek phallic god Priapus was transformed by Romans into the god Fascinus, both penetrative protector and conqueror. Black masculine iconicity is then about failure to be anything other than a phallus; the phallus always already speaks the man, and this is even the case for iconic Black men such as US American model Tyson Beckford and British Rugby player Maro Itoje.

Reading Black male iconicity: Beckford and Itoje

Male fashion week produces a contradiction as the male body and fashion seem incompatible. This is the case even when fashion has been at the forefront of the depiction of male bodies and the film industry has followed suit (Bordo, 2000). Within this display of men's bodies on catwalks and advertising, homo- and trans-phobia are at work in the taboos against feminized display and willing submission because both are incompatible with being a 'real man' (Bordo, 2000). Further, men as vulnerable and exposed to the sexualizing gaze whether from straight women or gay men or bi-women/-men make Black male models like Tyson Beckford objects to be consumed. He is marked as different and 'delectable' (Woodard, 2014; Figure 3.6) because of his unique looks drawn from his Black Panamanian father and his African/Chinese Jamaican mother. Black body consumerism, male fitness and beauty culture, which denies female vanity, male femininity and the taboo against the display of the male body, mean that Beckford continues to be portrayed as a very masculine 'rock' rather than a feminized 'leaner' (Bordo, 2000). The Black male supermodel, now in his 40s, has a net worth of $14 million. The message of his muscular body and darker skin continues to be challengingly aggressive, powerful and emotionally impenetrable. He is portrayed, in fact, as what Susan Bordo describes as 'face off masculinity'. This is the expected location of the Black man's

Figure 3.6 Model Tyson Beckford on stage at the Africa Rising Festival at the Royal Albert Hall, Kensington Gore, London, PA Images/Alamy.

body in a racialization which sets him as the hypermasculine and hypersexual object of desire whether straight, bi-sexual, gay, asexual or queer.

We also see this face off masculinity in *Tattler* magazine's October 2018 issue 'Sports Luxe Fashion' with the cover of Maro Itoje and Lady Amelia Windsor and its accompanying promotional video. Darker-skinned six-foot-five-inches tall Maro Itoje was then 26 years old, a second row forward for Saracens rugby team and England player. Lady Amelia Windsor is slightly built, white and the granddaughter of the Duke of Kent, a member of the British Royal Family. The video shot on the beach at Camber Sands in the summer shows Amelia in a big top over swimwear and Maro in shorts and a top and then topless on the beach. He shows his physical strength and very well-defined, muscular physique – lifting her, her on his back – agility by sprinting and playing with a rugby ball, 'fake' arm wrestling and jumping on one leg, before running on the beach together. He is a well-oiled, muscular, masculine sports machine, and she is emblematic for frail, white, aristocratic, femininity. This comparison repeats on the cover where she reclines dressed on his bare chest as they both face the camera with expressionless faces. Although her clothed back touches his bare, warm dark skin, they are detached from each other on the cover. What these images of Itojo as only body, athletic machine, dark-skinned prop for white feminine aristocratic frailty elide, is that he is a person. For example, he has a Black anti-racist mindset as we see in the *Guardian* (8/5/2021) 'How Rugby Star Maro Itoje Found His Voice' article by Jonathan Liew which says, 'From highlighting Black history to tackling everyday racism, the powerful athlete is determined to use his platform for change'.

The representations of Itoje and Beckford bring to mind Orlando Patterson's (1982) work on enslavement and social death. In his discussion in 'Authority, Alienation and Social Death', Patterson (1982) asserts that private and public symbols are a major source of power in the master-slave relationship enabling the social death of the enslaved who were introduced into the master's community as non-beings. The liminality of social death produced Black institutionalized marginality where the only use of the enslaved was 'through and for the master' (Patterson, 1982). For Cedric Robinson (2019: 187), speaking of People of African Descent, 'once captive in the domain of the historical systems of the West, it was not an issue of who we had been really or who we are really but what we could be made to be'. As we see from the example of Beckford and Itoje, they have been made to be the Black hypermasculine object of the white supremacist gaze as their bodies are consumed. Robinson's 'what we could be made to be', still persists 'in theoretical and historical deceptions which lead to the refabrications of racial discourse' within the capitalist world system which was profoundly affected by race ideology (Robinson, 2019: 187). Beckford's and Itoje's skins are caught in a web of profound anti-Blackness. For Christina Sharpe (2016: 7), in the US, such pervasive anti-Blackness produces Black life lived near death. We should extend this scope to include the Western Hemisphere, as this is the Black condition today because of the extension 'of the state of capture and subjection [of the plantation] in as many legal and extralegal ways as possible, into the present' (Sharpe, 2016: 12).

In *The Man-Not: Race, Class, Genre and the Dilemmas of Black Manhood*, Tommy Curry (2017: 1) asserts that, 'America makes corpses of Black men. It is simply the reality of our day that Black men die'. *The Black man* is denied the masculine multiplicity that is assumed by men racialized as white. This is the case as, 'hypermasculinity is proposed as the phylogenic marker of Black maleness' and 'Black males are thought to be the exemplifications of white (bourgeois) masculinity's pathological excess' (Curry, 2017: 2). Black men are thought in terms of threat, aggression, lack of intelligence, for example, and that has been how they have been constructed since enslavement's racist depictions. Black male death in the US 'is the boundary between the abject and the corpse the Black male inhabits' (Curry, 2017: 4). Paradoxically, in an anti-Black world, Black men are 'denied maleness and ascribed as feminine in relation to white masculinity [because Black maleness] lacks the power

of white masculinity [...] and is in fact a degendered negation of white maleness that is feminine because of its subordinate position' (Curry, 2017: 5–6). However, Black maleness
is not femaleness because it does not correspond with either
white maleness or femaleness. Thus, the Black man 'experiences the world as "*Man-Not*" [...] negated not from an origin
of (human) being, but from nihility [...] Non-being expresses
the condition of Black male being [...] rooted in the colonial formulation of sex designation not gender' (Curry, 2017:
6–7). This means that Black maleness is not 'synonymous to
the formulation of masculinity, or patriarchy, offered by white
reality' (Curry, 2017: 7). Anti-Black maleness as phobia drives
the physical violence of white supremacy.

Conclusion

The discussion has thought through the Black body as a raced
and gendered object in fashion and racism, as well as modelling
as global aesthetic labour. In doing this, white aesthetics and
fashion were decentred by looking at fashion from the viewpoint of the Western Hemispheric South. This highlighted the
syncretic nature of fashion itself established through the routes
of colonialism and contemporary global markets in racial capitalism, whether of objects like cloth marked as 'racial property'
or of bodies marked as 'different', 'exotic', 'unique to their
kind'. The fashion industry and modelling as global aesthetic
labour trades in and keeps biological racial categories alive
because of how it can draw on the affective life of race and
racism through the 'spectacle of the other' (Hall, 1997). The
spectacle of the other is produced from a position of privilege
that in turn enables 'eating the other' (hooks, 2014). 'Eating
the other' is also relevant for Black men being seen as priapic,
being constructed as hypersexual and being marked for death.
The spectacle of the other produces/draws on affects such as
fascination and hate as part of the intersectional anti-Black racism which animates the global fashion industry today where
'the look' is not race neutral. Rather, 'the look' in the Global
Northwest is one of racial dissection which produces what it

expects to find. That is, markers of racial difference from the continuing aesthetic ideal. The next chapter continues this analysis by looking at fear–hate and Black men's bodies.

Notes

1 An early version of this chapter was written with Ian law.
2 Priyan Elan 'Beverly Johnson calls for Condé Nast to interview Black people for senior roles' The Guardian, June 17, 2020.

4 White fear-hate of Black men's bodies

Masculinity and skin's affective politics

Introduction

Drawing on legal scholar Paul Butler's (2017) 'the chokehold' and literary critic Darieck Scott's (2010) 'extravagant abjection', Jared Sexton (2018) introduces the problematic of Black masculinity in all its complexity within an anti-Black world. Here Black masculinity is always something extraordinary and extra ordinary, never un-remarkable (Sexton, 2018). Instead, Black masculinity is noticeable as both hypermasculinity and hypomasculinity that mark its failure by being excessive in the case of the former or being the location of lack in the latter. For Sexton (2018), the crisis of the representation of Black masculinity in popular culture is that it is either too much or too little and bound by negative tropes such as the 'badman'. The badman instantiates the necessity for the chokehold. The chokehold is relevant for the experiences of all African American men and boys, 24/7, whether criminalized or not. This extends beyond US American life to encompass the Black Atlantic diaspora's many locations and nation states where 'controlling images' (Collins, 1990/2022) of Black men also persist and are continually recirculated. For example, Black men are constructed as 'muggers', 'drug dealers', 'comedians', 'being all brawn and no brain' and 'absent fathers'.

This chapter focuses on the chokehold of the libidinal economy of white fear-hate of Black men's bodies. It begins by drawing on Frank B. Wilderson 111's (2010) account of racialized libidinal

DOI: 10.4324/b23223-4

economies and Alexander Weheliye's (2014) work on racializing assemblages, to show that affect is important in understanding the location of Black masculine bodies as spaces of fear-hate. As this analysis unfolds, it unpacks other affects in the racialized libidinal economy such as guilt and derision. It then moves to look at how these affects' subterranean flow emerges through reproducing these bodies as objects that are always already 'known'. They are known through a white supremacist psychic frame of 'the sambo' because of continuing coloniality and its 'samboification' of society as a route to Black male containment (Tate, 2020). This leads to thinking samboification through George Yancy's (2008) work where he talks about the function of the white gaze of dissection as being to ensure white feelings of safety and tranquillity.

In order to flesh out this framing, the analysis will first look at contemporary 'white blackface' using the example of Justin Trudeau amongst others and the pleasure that emerges through its instantiation of relations of domination and anti-Black male hate. The chapter then moves to continuing to look at white pleasure through fear-hate in 'Black blackface' in 'the Black comedian' trope in the film *Jumanji* with Dwayne 'The Rock' Johnson and Kevin Hart, and in selected 'Old Spice' advertisements with Isaiah Mustafa and Terry Crews. Comedy's fear-hate sublimation is a precursor to the transracial consumption of Black men's bodies. The focus will be on the consumption of this white projection of the sublimated fear-hate of Black masculinities evinced in the diminution of threat through humour's continuing repetition of hate. Humour diminishes white fear of the black man's skin as much as it inscribes it with white hate by insistently re-drawing it with each repetition of the advertisement/filmic projection within the controlling image (Collins, 1990/2022) of 'the Black comedian'. Humour makes the affects of hate and fear both deniable within samboification. The chapter ends by thinking through lighter-skin male passing and 'border bodies' in the work of Black/white mixed-race actor Wentworth Miller in his feature debut film *The Human Stain* (2003) and the Fox television series *Prison Break* (2005–2017). Thinking through male passing and border bodies once again highlights Western Hemispheric racialized skin colour politics lived through fear-hate. It illustrates that the chokehold dictates that mixedness must be denied because having the skin appearance of whiteness brings bodies of value into being societally. This continues the reiteration of plantation race regimes. Let us move to looking at samboification's racialized assemblages and libidinal economies.

Racialized libidinal economies, racialized assemblages and the samboification of society

What we feel about Black men's skin colour results from both the racialization and gendering of the gaze. This interaction between skin and the intersectionality of race and gender means that we should not exclude libidinal and political economies in any discussion of the phenomenology of perception (Fanon, 2021) within racialized gender regimes and their imaginaries. Libidinal and political economies need to be focused on because power relations are significant in considerations of skin. Skin colour, texture, tone can make us approach some bodies because of affective attachment and even pass as someone else through them. Skin colour, texture, tone can be positive for affect and action in terms of attraction, alliance and love. Alongside the Black skin-philia that we get in contemporary and historical political movements like #SayHerName, #BLM, Black Power and Pan Africanism, skin can also be the site of repulsion, of Black skin-phobia. Black skin can be negatively affective when there is a turn to violence, hatred and appropriative consumption (Wilderson 111, 2010). The libidinal economy of Black men's skin operates within and through the political economy of anti-Black racism's misandry.

Frank B. Wilderson 111 (2010: 7) avers that racialized libidinal economies are affective, and although impacted by structures of feeling, they go beyond that to very mobile transmissions of affect that are societally fixated on this or that body and on this or that body part:

> [L]ibidinal economy functions variously across scales and is as 'objective' as political economy. It is linked not only

to forms of attraction, affection, and alliance, but also to aggression, destruction, and the violence of lethal consumption [...] it is the whole structure of psychic and emotional life [...] something more than but inclusive of or traversed by [...] a 'structure of feeling'; it is a dispensation of energies, concerns, points of attention, anxieties, pleasures, appetites, revulsions, phobias capable of great mobility and tenacious fixation.

Anti-Black man hate did not appear out of thin air. As I have said previously in looking at coloniality, enslavement, indenture and anti-Blackness, it was constructed by the white colonial psyche and its racist projections. It has been centuries in the making, through the Indigenous genocide and dispossession of white settler colonialism, plantation economy enslavement and indenture and their afterlives. Anti-Black man hate exists within and permeates the socio-cultural, politico-economic and affective context, that is, the racialized libidinal economies, of the Western Hemisphere. Anti-Black man hate is structural, systemic, institutionalized and hardwired into Western Hemispheric life. This means that anti-Black misandry is not reducible to isolated incidents enacted by marginalized individuals. Instead, anti-Black misandry is normalized right across Western Hemispheric societies (Curry, 2017, 2021) which we see reflected in higher rates of incarceration, deaths at the hands of the police, over-representation in mental health institutions and over-policing, for example. Anti-Black misandry reflects the hegemonic values of the status quo of Black men's subjection.

Anti-Black misandry reflects hegemonic values and produces these racist effects through particular performative work which amplifies the fear-hate dynamic in relation to its target. The affective life of anti-Black misandry emerges as the latter 'recreate[s] the threatened (real or imaginary) hegemony of the [white] perpetrator's group, and the "appropriate" subordinate [Black man] identity of the victim's group [...] to re-establish their "proper" relative positions, as given and reproduced by broader ideologies [...] of social and political inequality' (Perry, 2004: 128). Understood as systemic and institutionalized (Hadreas, 2007), we can see anti-Black man hate working within the social processes, routine daily encounters and institutions of ordinary social life to reproduce 'appropriate' socio-political, cultural and economic subordination.

Peter Hadreas (2007: 2–3) outlines the contours of hate as social process and how this is embedded in institutions and social processes which we can also see in operation in anti-Black misandry

> First, there is a degree of generalization. [...] Second, an exclusive *or* [...] increasingly more intense degrees of generality and 'either-or' opposition appear. A limiting case of hatred emerges when groups of people are believed to be monolithically *necessarily* worthy of harm and blame. [...] [Black men are] made into sub-humans, who [...] seek to undermine the home-group. [...] The development of such hatred [...] may be abetted by [...] political propaganda as well as the opportunity hatred provides for avoiding self-doubt, fear and humiliation.

Generalization, an exclusive or, being 'monolithically necessarily worthy of harm' as sub-humans, 'the principle of blame' or 'the extra-vituperative principle' entailing a shifting of blame for hate to those that are hated (Hadreas, 2007), and the haters' need for personal cohesiveness as superior, underlie the structure of feeling (Wilderson 111, 2010; Williams, 1977) of anti-Black man hate. Notice also that anti-Black man hate is necessary for the warding off of fear and other affects and dispositions of 'white fragility' (Di Angelo, 2019). Anti-Black man hate allied with white fragility textures Black men's bodies as knowable and known 'flesh' (Spillers, 2003; Weheliye, 2014) for sale within global racial capitalism's (Robinson, 2019) necropolitical (Mbembe, 2019) life of our intersubjective world riven by racialized inequity.

This process of producing and recycling knowable and known hated flesh enables those racialized as white and those Black and People of Colour affiliated with white supremacy to remain superior, to avoid white fragility's (Di Angelo, 2019) self-doubt, fear and humiliation. Anti-Black misandry, like misogynoir, keeps the system of anti-Blackness alive, active and inimical to Black life. The very ordinariness of anti-Black man hate means that we all understand its contours because we share the same set of North Atlantic universals (Truillot, 2015), whether we are attached to them or vigorously contest them. These North Atlantic universals are dispersed continually through the slipstream of cultural production in the Black Atlantic diaspora and beyond. That is why we understand how anti-Black male hate works through stereotypes, epistemologies of ignorance (Mills, 1997, 2007), violence and death at the hands of the state.

For Jared Sexton (2018), the public treats Black people with hate and fear, routinely humiliating them, with gender, age, sexuality, ability, class, for example, adding to structural vulnerability. The late bell hooks (2003) asserts that this libidinal economy marks Black men and boys as unloved in a society in which they have been failed by white and Black leaders, and they are surrounded societally by envy, desire and hate. The socio-political psyche of anti-Black misandry is one which is indeed twisted if we look at the affects entailed as hate is paired with desire and envy. Desire for the other as consumable inferior object and envy of that consumable inferior object in whole (for example, athletic ability) or in part (for example, muscles, penis) illustrate the paradoxes of anti-Blackness where the surface desire for Blackness can have envy and hate so very closely aligned that they can be activated without drawing breath. Think, for example, about white male sexual desire for Black others and the brutalities meted out to fulfil this during enslavement and colonialism.

According to Tommy Curry (2017: 26), '[C]anonical gender theory' assertions that 'Black men –even when shown [in colonialism] to have been victims of rape, economic marginality, medical experimentation, cannibalism, and castration [...] only answer to their victimization [...] is in fact, (white) patriarchy'. In his view, Black males do not simply aspire to white colonial patriarchy but rather developed a tradition of manhood 'erected on the foundations of ethnology that was anti-imperial, anticolonial, and, consequently, not [white] patriarchal' (Curry, 2017: 26).

Curry's assertions problematize the Eurocentrism, colonial origin and utilization of gender because these make it inapplicable to Blackness. This is supported by Oyèrónké Oyewúmì's (1997) work on gender in pre-colonial and colonial Yorubaland. Therefore, what is important for this book is understanding that what we study when we speak of, or analyze, representations of black men, is 'negations of (*white*) *MAN* itself' (Curry, 2017: 27). Analyzing these negations in cultural representations risk reproducing Black men as meat, insensate flesh, or as 'undifferentiated Black phallic flesh' (Curry, 2017: 29). 'Merely seeing the body of the black male differentiates it from that of a white man (humanity) and separates it in kind from the phylogeny of the human. The Black male is defined by this distance to MAN, his nature being replaced with that of brute and savage; he is made into horror' (Curry, 2017: 34).

For example, 'the badman' as a site of fear is an active racist stereotype. It spreads out as a discursive 'second skin' (Cheng, 2011) to encompass the bodies of *all* Black men constructed as flouting laws, criminal and endangering the possibility of Black communal and individual uplift and advancement. Black men and boys – as those who will already be younger versions of badmen – then live in the shadow of this myth surrounded by ambivalent affects. These ambivalent affects include love/hatred, desire/fear, attachment/aversion, for example. The terror that is the Black man 'is not solely racial apathy; it also includes a very real sexual appetency' (Curry, 2017: 34). As we have seen, fear-hate also aligns with desire. The myth of the badman which necessitates the imposition of the chokehold in US society means that Black men and boys have to demonstrate that they are not a threat to the public and the police, whilst being treated as a perpetual threat irrespective of class, ethnicity, age, ability, sexuality and gender expression/identity, for example.

We can see the badman chokehold in which Black men exist in a racist incident in New York Central Park's 'the Ramble' on May 25, 2020. A Black male avid birdwatcher, Christian Cooper, a Harvard graduate who works in communications and is on the board of the New York City Audubon Society, challenged a white woman, Amy Cooper, who had let her dog off the lead. Her response was to call the police and make it clear that an African American man was threatening her, deploying racist stereotypes. Mr Cooper filmed her actions. She was charged in July 2020 with making a false report, one of the few times that a white person in the US has faced a criminal charge for wrongfully making a police complaint against a Black person (Sarah Maslin Nir 'How 2 Lives Collided in Central Park, Rattling the Nation' *The New York Times* June 14, 2020). She subsequently lost her job. This was not the police or a state organ but a white woman deploying the chokehold using a centuries' old trope of Black men as physical threats to white women. Christian Cooper could only escape from this racist lie by filming and posting their encounter online. The chokehold extends to the public, and Black men must show that they are not threats in their very being (Sexton, 2018) and comportment. The chokehold comes from the phobic threat projected onto Black men and boys and Black masculinity, however and whenever it appears (Sexton, 2018). 'As a phobogenic entity, the Black male is liable for the anxiety other individuals experience […] He is culpable for the violence these groups imagine, for their delusions as if they are actual. This shared neurosis often leads to the rationalization of Black male death in America' (Curry, 2017: 36) White neurosis, anxiety, hate-fear are aspects of the anti-Black male libidinal economy that facilitates and maintains symbolic, systemic and epistemic violence.

We can see this libidinal economy through the contemporary life of a colonial artefact of the white psyche, that is, sambo. In its enactments and representations, sambo still attempts to subjugate Black diasporic communities as a transcultural North Atlantic Universal which everyone understands even if it might have different names, like the gollywog (UK), Sarotti- Moor (Austria) and Zwarte Piet (the Netherlands) (Tate, 2020a: 5):

> [S]ambo is understood only through a range of concepts with the common denominator being its position on a 'lower moral and ontological position' on the racial hierarchy (Mills, 2007). Indeed, sambo is positioned as non-human to the extent that whiteness was seen as

co-extensive with humanity. This produced common attributes across white European settler colonies that continue to resist erasure of empire's governance and governmentality. sambo was part of a colonial reason which became common sense within empire's citation of subjection in its colonial and ongoing archives of infra-human kind in which everyday racism is conjoined with the politics of states structured through racial dominance. (Post) colonial European states attempt to erase their sambo past in the present through concealment, erasure, silencing and 'epistemologies of white ignorance' (Mills, 1997) when sambo is so cemented into the psyche, folklore and popular culture that it refuses being consigned to oblivion.

We have to remember that sambo has many forms as we see in the previous examples. We also see sambo in the US 'coon' and the blackface minstrel globally. It still exists today because of the embeddedness of Symbolic sambo as a shortcut to describing the Black body and character in opposition to the 'implicit cultural blanchitude which had been central to the social machine of the world system' (Wynter, 1979: 150). Symbolic sambo remains part of anti-Blackness in the 21st century because it 'was necessary to the self-conception not only of the master, but to that of all whites in the [US] South who patterned their own self-conception on the master-model' (Wynter, 1979: 150). Although Wynter situates sambo in the US enslavement South, sambo has travelled far from that through the roots and routes of colonialism, enslavement and coloniality. It is now global as a 'second skin' (Cheng, 2011), a marker of subjection, the very naming of white domination of another as flesh, a signifier of thingification and location of racist derision. Let us then add derision to our list of affects within the anti-Black libidinal economy. Anti-Black derision has always been a mainstay of racist humour. It draws on stereotypes and seeks to inferiorize racialized others. Therefore, laughing along and not calling out the humour as racist is 'ideological denial' (Weaver, 2010: 537). We see this continuing ideological denial in the support for and use of white blackface.

White blackface

White blackface is pervasive even today. This continues to draw from 'the most notorious and arguably the most influential instance of racechange – one that still remains taboo because of its overt racism – [which] appeared on the nineteenth-century minstrel stage, where white actors ridiculed African Americans' (Gubar, 1997: 11). An anti-Black libidinal economy dependent on sambo/gollywog/wog/coon/minstrel tropes keeps Black subjection through humour alive in Canada (Howard, 2018) and globally (Lhamon Jr., 1989; Lott, 1991, 1993; Roediger, 1999; Tate, 2020). Some examples from the UK, the US and Canada will suffice to support this assertion.

In the UK in 2021, when Yorkshire Cricket was embroiled in the racism claims made by British Asian cricketer Azeem Rafiq, English cricketer Alex Hales apologized for dressing up in blackface in 2009 to imitate his 'musical hero' Tupac Shakur. He said, 'I obviously realize that this is incredibly disrespectful and I want to apologize for the offence this has no doubt caused. It was incredibly reckless on my behalf. I want to apologize for that, apologize to the club for the embarrassment it will have caused them' (London Evening Standard, November 19, 2021, 'Hales Says Sorry for "Incredibly Reckless and Foolish" Black-Face Photo' – Will Macpherson). Coventry South (UK) Member of Parliament Zarah Sultana faced an online racist attack in 2021 when she was told to go back to her country: '[Y]ou are in my country not yours, you do not belong here…blackfacing bothers you, TOUGH, one of OUR traditions, it is NOT for us to consider you. Britain First rising, we will soon get out [sic] heritage back and tough if you don't like it'. (Coventry Telegraph, November 15, 2021, 'Coventry MP Zarah Sultana Faces Online Racial Attack Telling Her to "Go Back to Her Country": The Vile Email Said She Did "Not Belong Here" and Stated That Blackface Was "Tradition"' – Latifa Yedroudj).

The comedy film *Tropic Thunder* (2008, Director Ben Stiller, Red Hour Productions/DreamWorks Pictures; Figure 4.1) parodied war films, including those based on the Vietnam War, and grossed $195.7 million. White actor Robert Downey Jr played

Figure 4.1 Tropic thunder original movie poster, SilverScreen/Alamy.

Kirk Lazarus, an Australian actor who underwent an extreme transformation to become an African American soldier for his part in the movie. This is an example of racial cosplay/'black-fishing' aimed at a white audience who might see 'the joke' and laugh at it (Tate, 2021). Indeed, we can see this as an example of 'post-race' anti–Black racism (Tate, 2021). This assertion is supported by Lazarus saying at one point, 'I know who I am. I'm a dude, playing a dude disguised as another dude' to make it plain that this is not his skin but one that he has assumed like Hilary/Ruby in *Lovecraft Country*. He can always go back to being a white Australian after making a profit through blackface comedy, a position which many in a white audience who see blackface as harmless fun would also share. In a scene from the movie that they were shooting, Tugg Speedman (Ben Stiller) says, 'I don't believe you people'. Kirk Lazarus (in blackface) responds, 'What do you mean, "you people"?' This is a response to be expected from Black people in answer to the white racist affront 'you people'. In response to Lazarus, Black actor Alpa Chino (already assumed to be funny in its take on the name of actor Al Pacino) (Brandon T. Jackson), asks Lazarus, 'What do *you* mean "you people"?' This 'humorous' exchange brings us back to the fact of Lazarus' whiteness and his blackface performance of a Black man as the joke. I say 'humorous' here because white blackface is not at all funny to audiences being targeted by racist disparaging humour, and we see this in Alpa Chino's pointed 'What do *you* mean..?' The '*you*' unmasks Lazarus' white blackface and undermines the possibility that Lazarus who un-problematically wore blackface was asking a political, anti-racist activist question.

In 2020 in Canada, the Kamloops Royal Canadian Mounted Police looked into Constable Rupert Meinke's Instagram posts after he made blackface jokes while having a black face mask applied which he called a 'Black face session', followed by, 'is my skin care racist? Micro aggressions matter' (kamloopsthisweek. com July 5, 2020). Justin Trudeau, Canada's prime minister wore blackface makeup and dressed as Aladdin for an Arabian Nights–themed party at a private school, West Point Grey Academy, where he taught in 2001. This was among a series of photos released of him in blackface. There are at least three photos and one video of Trudeau in blackface. When he was in high school at Montreal's Collège Jean-de-Brébeuf, he wore blackface to sing Harry Belafonte's "Day-O". As the images surfaced, Trudeau held an emergency news conference on his campaign plane, apologizing and saying he should have known better. He said, 'It was something that I didn't think was racist at the time, but now I recognize it was something racist to do and I am deeply sorry' (CBC News, 2019). At least he has moved past Canadian insistence that white blackface is just harmless fun, and we should get over it to move forward, even whilst it continues in Halloween parties, campus carnivals, frosh events, sporting events, comedy fests, theatre performances and comedy revues (Howard, 2018).

Drawing on Saidiya Hartman (1997), Philip Howard (2018) discusses the relationship between anti-Blackness, Black embodiment and white pleasure in order to see how black-face is 'funny' to its white practitioners and audiences. Humour advances racist ideas while denying racism (Howard, 2018), for example, blackface being worn because you are a white fan of Tupac. What we see in blackface is intense attention to the body, to dark skin, 'big lips', 'googly eyes', the very archetype of blackness produced by the white colonial psyche which contin-ues in contemporary 'post-race' coloniality's blackface of Bob Marley, Usain Bolt and weed smoking dreadlocked 'Jamaican yardie criminals'. The humour of blackface is the embodied racism that continues to ensure white dominance, therefore, facilitating white pleasure in proximity to Black bodies much as it did during enslavement (Howard, 2018). This anti-Black libidinal economy's derision rooted in enslavement left a legacy of anti-Black humour that continues to instrumentalize Black embodiment today as a construct of the white imagination. (This white imagined construct therefore needs to be concep-tualized as black and blackness to distinguish this from Black as political, social, cultural and psychic identification from within Blackness itself). The (white) pleasure experienced is because of the (white) presentation of the Black body where a white body is expected (Howard, 2018). Whites do not only tell jokes about Black people but 'become the joke by wearing the Black body' through darkened skin. The 'pleasure of blackface' draws on the 'power and violence of racialized social relations' and on the 'deniability' of racism where 'explicit racist discourses can be nominally disapproved of' (Howard, 2018).

Lewis Ricardo Gordon (2014) gives us another take on white blackface when he speaks about the affects attached to Negrophobia. He states that when we hear the word 'black', or in this case see its racist parody on a white body, it develops and continues the imposed reality of Black communities' lives. The imposed reality of white blackface is formed through the colonial construction of 'the Negro' in the 'imagination of a world that transformed millions of people in Africa into what Oliver Cox [2000] called the proletarian race' (Gordon, 2014: 181). The anti-Blackness embedded in white blackface reflects whiteness as a structure of domination seeking protection from an imagined object that turns out to be [its] own projection. Thus, the Negro threat was in fact an expression of a wish not to be held responsible for [the] desire [for white supremacy]. Yet, such self-concealment often carries guilt, which demands justification in a multitude of depictions. (Gordon, 2014: 181) Here, we have another addition to the anti-Black libidinal economy's affects, white guilt. Whites also labour under the supposition of Black desire for whiteness (Gordon, 2014). This is foundational in the narcissistic investment in the white intersectional self which also entails another supposition. That is, that Black people want to be part of a system in which they are inferiorized and governed by whiteness. Black inferiorization occurs through the supposition of the 'happy Negro' of the plantation who understands that it is not good to be 'a Negro' (Gordon. 2014). This is the Negro loved by whiteness, 'if by that affection we understand a narcissistic investment in a false image. While there is hatred of Black people there is a pervasive love of Negroes' (Gordon' 2014: 183). This love of the white sambo projection *only* is another element of the anti-Black libidinal economy.

The hatred that is foundational to anti-Blackness and the love of the white constructed Negro image/sambo brings to mind what Stuart Hall (1997) talks about as a 'racialized regime of representation'. This regime rests on stereotypes drawn from enslavement and colonialism that persisted in the 20th century and still exist today, even though they have been and still are contested by Black liberation struggles. Stereotypes are imagined as much as they are perceived as 'real' (Hall, 1997). Stereotypes essentialize and fix racial difference using a strategy of splitting, which divides the 'normal' from the 'abnormal', expelling anything which does not fit the stereotype itself (Hall, 1997). Through splitting, stereotypes maintain a social and symbolic racialized gender order, setting up a symbolic boundary between an imagined (white) us and racialized others. These others become dangerous, even taboo, and negative affect clusters around them because of power inequalities that enable symbolic power in representations to negatively mark and classify Black bodies.

This is clear from the previous examples of white blackface. What we also see in white blackface and will see in the following discussion on Black blackface is that what is 'visually produced by representation is only half of the story. The other half – the deeper meaning – lies in *what is not being said, but is being fantasized, what is implied but cannot be shown*' (Hall, 1997: 263). Stereotyping involves fantasy and projection, and we see this in terms of how skin, especially its colour, is used as a substitute for whole human beings as Fanon (2021) shows. Fanon (2021) says that he is not the slave of an idea that others have of him but a slave to his appearance. Reading this assertion Wilderson 111 (2010: 37) states:

> [B]eing can thus be thought of in the first ontological instance, as non-niggerness, and slavery then as niggerness. [...] The visual field 'my own appearance' is the cut, the mechanism that elaborates the division between the non-niggerness and slavery, the difference between the living and the dead. Skin is that visual field, the organic 'mechanism' that dictates the contours of the living and the dead.

Skin replaces a whole person through the effect 'of the representational practice of fetishism' where fantasy intervenes in representation in relation to 'what cannot be seen, what cannot be shown' (Hall, 1997: 266). Fantasy substitutes an object – in this case skin – 'for a dangerous, powerful, or forbidden force' (Hall, 1997: 266). We see this in the transracial consumption of Black men's bodies in Black blackface film and advertising, for example.

Black blackface and transracial consumption of Black men's bodies: *Jumanji* and Old Spice

For Frantz Fanon (2021), the Black man must be black in relation to the white man. This relation between Blackness and whiteness hardwired into the psyches, societies, politics and knowledge systems in the Western Hemisphere means that the Black man has no 'ontological resistance' in the eyes of the white man. Hortense Spillers (2003) makes a similar observation when she says that the Black woman in the US is necessary for the white woman to come into being. For both Spillers and Fanon, race is a rigid bifurcation. Further, the projection of Black skin produced through what for Fanon is the psychic and phenomenological experience of the historico-racial schema is necessary for white skin to come into being. This occurs through commodity racism. The late bell hooks already warned us about this when she said that commodification erases critical consciousness and, as such, the possibility of liberation because resistance is replaced by consumption. However, what happens when Black men wear blackface? For whom and to whom are they recognizable? Does this continue colonialism's 'black man' in relation to whiteness?

We see this Black blackface problematic in the past dispute between rappers Drake and Pusha-T. Pusha-T circulated an old photograph of Drake in blackface, leaving Drake to explain that the old picture of him was a complaint about the lack of work for Black actors (Tate, 2020a: 152). However, what Drake should have remembered is that:

> the 21st century white sambo psyche thinks that their construction, sambo, resides behind blackface. That sambo's mask does not hide anything else but its construction of Black and People of Colour's inferiority. Drake should have recalled that racial capitalism's negativity lies in the fact that it reinforces commodification of racial identity, that it degrades it by reducing it to a commodity to be sold, bought and consumed. His blackface caused resentment because Black people felt exploited, demeaned by white supremacy as Drake seemed to be reproducing their racist stereotypes, their domination, their Black social death through the continuing samboification of social life.
> (Tate, 2020a: 153)

We should not only look at Drake and blame him for perpetuating negative stereotypes. We are presented regularly with Black men wearing blackface without the need for the minstrel burned cork and makeup in advertising and Hollywood's dream factory. Both of these venues for Black male representation still keep serving up the white construction of the 'minstrel coon'/'dandy coon'/'sambo' as comedic, the black 'cocksman', 'picaninny', black men as 'all brawn no brain buffoon' and 'the badass' (Yuen, 2017).

Nancy Wang Yuen (2017) looks at the typecasting of actors of colour in Hollywood. In her view, actors of colour are honoured in awards ceremonies 'for playing slaves, maids and criminals rather than civil rights leaders, the Academy denies them the full breath of accolades afforded to white actors. Even if the Academy does not vote to keep Blacks in 'their place' there is a record of a pattern of bias' (Yuen, 2017: 4) She also speaks of the typecasting in Hollywood impacting the lowest-paid actors to the top-paid stars. If an actor has been successful in a particular role, they will keep being cast in that role to maximize profit and minimize the risk of movies making a financial loss (Yuen, 2017). This is the basis of typecasting where actors are cast in a limited repertoire of roles based on race, gender, physical traits and previous roles (Yuen, 2017). An example of this is 'the badass', a stereotypical portrayal of Black men from the Blaxploitation era films of the 1970s, for example, Samuel L. Jackson in the action comedy *Shaft* (2019, Director Tim Story). Typecasting normalizes whiteness as a skin universal capable of limitless repertoires while recycling Black stereotypes. I will look at some of these 'controlling images' (Collins, 1990/2022) of Black men in my discussion of the following examples of visual representation in films and advertising.

In *Jumanji: Welcome to the Jungle* (2017, Director Jake Kasdan; Figure 4.2), four high school students, Spencer (Alex Wolff), Fridge (Ser'Darius Blain), Martha (Morgan Turner) and Bethany (Madison Iseman), are in detention. While serving detention they choose to be characters in a video game and get sucked into the dangerous world of Jumanji. They have to finish the game to escape and have three lives marked in black bars on their forearms. Bethany becomes Sheldon Oberon (Jack Black), palaeontologist, archaeologist, cartographer, and Martha becomes Ruby Roundhouse (Karen Gillan) 'killer of men' and dance fighting expert. We see two stereotypes of the black man in circulation in the film through the vehicle of comedy. 'The spectacular, fantastic action hero', Dr Smolder

Figure 4.2 Jumanji: Welcome to the Jungle 2017 film with from left: Nick Jonas, Dwayne Johnson, Karen Gillan, Jack Black, Kevin Hart, Pictorial Press Ltd/Alamy.

Bravestone (Dwayne 'The Rock' Johnson), archaeologist and explorer – transformed from Spencer Gilpin a white, skinny, neurotic, germophobe, allergy suffering, EpiPen user, high school nerd who is a video game fanatic. We also see 'the piccaninny', Franklin 'Mouse' Finbar (Kevin Hart), converted into a diminutive zoologist and weapons valet in the game from Fridge, a high school football player who gets Spencer to do his homework so he can stay on the football team. The film grossed over $962 million worldwide. Black blackface sells well globally by representing *the* blackness that is known through endlessly circulating stereotypes.

The comedy begins when Bravestone and Finbar drop into the jungle in Jumanji as action hero and sidekick. Bravestone looks around for the others and looking surprised says, 'I don't sound like this, where is my hair?' However, he is amazed by and pleased with his bulky, tall, muscular (light-skinned Black) body. Interestingly, throughout the entire movie, no mention is made of the racial skin swop that has occurred from Spencer to The Rock. As the others fall into the jungle (Fridge) Finbar asks, 'Where is the rest of me?' in reference to his diminution. The contrast in size between Fridge and Spencer is also made humorous when they are chased by Van Pelt's (Bobby Cannavale) motorbike gang and Spencer gives Fridge a piggyback because he is too slow. Spencer is clearly the leader in the game, as he is the only character to whom all of the game guides relate. No one else is spoken to by the game guides, and no one else is called 'mighty hero', or told, 'Jumanji needs you'. We are reminded of Spencer's Jewish ethnicity at a few points in the film. One of these is when he uses the Yiddish phrase 'Oy vey' to show his dismay, following a tense moment produced by their young male bazaar guide's (Rohan Chand) statement, 'What you need is in the basket. One wrong move you'll be in a casket. Trust one another and never blink. The missing piece is not what you think'. The other is when they are drinking margaritas made by Alex Vreeke 'Seaplane' (Nick Jonas) who has been in the game for 20 years and has only one life left, and he says 'l'chaim' when they toast. The humour of these reminders of his ethnicity reassures the film's audience that Spencer has just done a skin swop for the game and his white skin, psyche and identity remain intact.

We see the hero–sidekick relation as one of diminutive Finbar challenging very big Bravestone throughout the film, especially when tensions run high. For example, Fridge (Finbar) asserts his dislike of Spencer (Bravestone) in a scene where they are walking along the side of a cliff. Spencer is clearly afraid of heights because he clings to the rock wall of the cliff as he slowly inches forward while the others walk at a regular pace facing forward. Fridge dislikes Spencer because he has been kicked off the football team as a result of Spencer plagiarising himself when he did Fridge's homework. Fridge asserts that it is all Spencer's fault and says, 'I should kick the shit out of you right now'. Spencer looks confused and looks at his body and back at Fridge, 'I'd like to see you try'. Fridge eyes Spencer from head to toe, 'Oh, ok, I see what's going on here. Oh, you think because you what? 6'4, 6'5, 270 pounds ah pure muscle I'm supposed to be afraid of you? Is that what you think?' Spencer again looks confused and says, 'Maybe'. Fridge walks up to him, only getting halfway up his chest, and says, 'Let me tell you sumn, you're still the same annoying kid that I've been trying to shake since 7th grade. Ain't nuthin changed'. Spencer looks upset and Fridge says, 'Don't let this new body get your butt whopped'. Fridge goes towards Spencer who jumps back and calls Fridge 'Dumbass'. Fridge pushes Spencer off the cliff and he loses a life. Spencer comes back into the game with two lives left and Fridge pointing at him says, 'Don't call me a dumbass'. Spencer retorts, 'Don't push me' walking towards Fridge who replies, 'Or what, Spencer?' Spencer says, 'I'll push you back' and Fridge lunges at Spencer pushing at his chest. Spencer remains unmoved. Fridge slaps Spencer and Spencer punches him into the rock wall but looks confused as if he did not know his own strength. Fridge responds, 'Did you just smack me? You smacked me?' Clenching his fist and looking upset, Spencer, correctly reading his fist as intention to fight, says, 'Fridge no'. Fridge punches at Spencer, who ducks out of the way and then ends up, saving Fridge from falling off the cliff by hanging onto his backpack. 'Don't let this new body get your butt whopped', speaks to who the real badman is irrespective of size and who should be feared. Not the superhero whose lighter skin covers the white body but the darker-skinned big Black man who morphs into a darker-skinned smaller Black man whose clothing and use of a way of speaking that the audience would read as Ebonics, already sets him up as a comedian. However, he also holds a grudge and can be deadly like other Black men.

Bravestone's strengths include smouldering intensity and he has no weaknesses. Finbar's strengths are zoology and being a weapons valet and his weaknesses are cake, speed and strength. Throughout the film, humour in the form of Spencer's fear, sexual inexperience, uncertainty and other weaknesses within a Black hypermasculine larger-than-life action hero/professor body with no weaknesses serves to make Bravestone relatable to the audience as a comedian. Further, he reprised the role of Robin Williams and that was probably a joke in itself, Black blackface where the white body is expected.

Both Bravestone and Finbar have two sides – teenagers Spencer and Fridge – which add interest and depth to the characters and encourage us to think about how fetishism works. Remember, for Hall (1997) fetishism involves disavowal. That is, a strategy through which to indulge and at the same time deny a powerful fascination, where 'what has been tabooed nevertheless finds a displaced form of representation' (Hall, 1997: 266). Fetishism both displays and hides the tabooed, dangerous or forbidden object of desire. In this case, the phallus, which is displaced by turning the gaze onto Bravestone's super-built body, even while we fear that it is still dangerously there. Bravestone could be related to another US American anti-Black male stereotype, the sambo/coon dandy who as a free Black man is a threat to gullible white women (Tate, 2020a). For example, we see this threat rehearsed in the US American white supremacist song 'The Negro and the Rising Man' (White, 1863: 54 cited in Tate, 2020a). 'The song warns gullible Southern women (belles) against "niggers" who assume new airs and graces that cover with perfume the fact that they are still sambo' (Tate, 2020a: 50). This stereotype is illustrated in his 'smouldering intensity' that white teenagers Bethany (Professor Shelly Oberon) and Martha (Ruby Roundhouse) are virtually overwhelmed by. This follows the fight with Fridge when Spencer says, 'Enough, we can't waste lives. We need each other. Like it or not, we have to do this together'. Bethany (Oberon) asks Spencer if the smoulder happens naturally or if it is controllable, to which he answers, 'It just happens naturally'. His strength in the game, smouldering intensity, is interesting if we look at smoulder. Smoulder means to 'burn sluggishly', to 'exist in a state of suppressed activity' and to 'show supressed anger, hate, jealousy'. Sluggishness and suppressed activity deny his hyper-masculine threat to the white women who are overcome by his smoulder, while the suppression of anger, hate, jealousy deny the powerful fascination with *the* black man which is integral to fetishism even whilst that man is in plain sight as the male lead.

The danger that Black hypersexuality poses to white women is dealt with in the film through humour in order to mitigate white fear but also to hide white hate. Here we have Spencer, a fearful weakling, transformed into the most coveted and desired hypermasculine body which he himself so revers that at the end of the game he says to Ruby (his love interest, Martha) that he does not want to leave but to continue living as Bravestone. We also see something else, the 'civilizing' of the Black man through literally absorbing, consuming whiteness, through bodily assimilating Spencer with his phobias, neuroses, fears and inhibitions. Spencer reduces Bravestone's positioning as spectacular action hero, through making him appear less masculine, less of a danger. We see this for example, in the moment of his confession to Ruby Roundhouse (Martha) that he likes her, that she reciprocates because she likes 'nerds'. Although he is Dr Bravestone, we only perceive the action hero. Ruby makes this clear when she does not see him as a nerd like Spencer. She is not bothered about bodies (and by projection the Black phallus), only intelligence. Displacing the gaze of the audience from phallus to muscle and then to (white) brain disavows the sexualizing nature of the gaze with its looking/not looking and ambivalent desire to be satisfied in finding its projected stereotype. 'All brawn and no brain', an archetype of Black men, does not appeal to this white woman. We also see the blunting of the danger of the Black phallus when their first kiss is a dismal, messy, disgusting-looking, failure. The kiss itself is only successful when Spencer and Martha as themselves kiss as the film is ending. What we see when we look through fetishism is a search for the illicit pleasure of Black hypermasculinity's failure and the possibility for its recuperation only through whiteness. The white saviour complex means that Black men continue to be the white man's burden as they were during colonialism and enslavement, and the black man is subjected to inferiorization within racialized skin hierarchies as we see in the figure of the 'picaninny'.

Figure 4.3 Christmas card greeting an American card about 1930, Pictorial Press Ltd/Alamy.

Fridge as Franklin 'Mouse' Finbar brings to mind the US 'picaninny' and what Stuart Hall (1997: 266) writing from the UK context calls, 'Black youth as sambo simpletons'. Picaninnies were depicted with animals whether farm or wild, such as in the 'Little Black Sambo' book with its tigers, and dark-skinned, red-lipped, big-eyed sambo. 'Picaninnies were child coons and the dominant racial caricature of Black children for much of US history' (www.ferris.edu 'The Picaninny Caricature'). According to Jayna Brown (2008: 24), picaninny comes from *picayune*, a small value coin circulated in the US in the 1800s that illustrates the 'interchangeability between the black child bodies and the small bits of money required for their acquisition. Slave children were living currency'. Much before this in the 1700s, Black women, children and men were in vogue as servants in the royal courts and well-to-do family homes of Russia, Sweden, Denmark, the UK and other parts of Europe. The mischievous, capering picaninnies grown on the plantations in the US South became 'stock characters of the popular press, the minstrel stage and the music score' (Brown, 2008: 26). Little Harry was the picaninny in Harriet Beecher Stowe's *Uncle Tom's Cabin* and in Moby Dick (1851), 'Pip' was 'the little Negro' working aboard the Pequod (Brown, 2008: 30). At the turn of the 20th century, the slave disappeared and the picaninny became a colonial subject through European and US American colonial expansion and empire building (Brown, 2008). In 1901, Black mezzo-soprano Belle Davis went on a tour of Britain's Empire Music halls and theatres with her own 'picaninny chorus', 7-year-old Fernandes 'Sonny' Jones and 9-year-old Irving 'Sneeze' Williams. They toured the UK, Europe and Scandinavia. In 1902, they were recorded by Gramophone Records in London, later appearing in a short film in Paris (Brown, 2008). There is a history of singer-led 'picaninny choruses' in Britain and Europe in the early 1900s, linking European tropes of happy enslaved Black children in their colonies to those of the US. 'Black children were considered to embody metonymically the condition of the lesser races, locked in a perpetual state of childlike simplicity, prone to excess, always emotional and immediate in their responses.

Their 'natural' behaviour was irrepressible physical and vocal expression' (Brown, 2008: 48).

This is a perfect description of Finbar (Fridge). It is this picaninny trope subconsciously called on by Hollywood without any need to be named that enables Finbar to be 'funny' globally in the 21st century for those who laugh at racist jokes. The only deviation from this trope is when it comes to his strength, zoology, even though this closeness to animals is also part of the picaninny, as previously stated. We see his animal knowledge reflected only when he defangs a snake, and recognizes and describes the snake, elephant, rhinos and jaguars. In the defanging scene in the bazaar, Spencer thinks that there might be a snake in the basket and is reluctant to do anything about it. Fridge says, 'Yep, sounds like a Bravestone thing to me'. Spencer replies, 'Why would this be a Bravestone thing?' Fridge retorts, 'Because you're the mighty hero. You heard what he said, Jumanji needs you. Now git'. Spencer fearfully says, 'I don't wanna do this', but opens the basket. When the snake appears, Fridge, with a panicked face, shouts 'Black Mamba', and Spencer hurriedly puts the lid back onto the basket. Fridge then quickly tells everyone about the snake, 'That's a Black Mamba. A quarter milligram of its venom is enough to kill an adult. You feel a tingling sensation in your mouth and extremities followed by a fever, foaming at the mouth and ataxia which means loss of muscle control'. The punchline that undermines his expert knowledge and makes him the joke follows, 'How do I know that?' When the snake lunges at Martha, Spencer grabs it by the head asking, 'What do I do?' In that moment, he gives up leadership temporarily to Fridge who is the zoology expert, who responds, 'Yuh gotta defang it'. Spencer's astonished, 'I gotta what?' is followed by Fridge talking through and completing the defanging of the snake, while Spencer looks overwhelmed. The scene ends with Fridge smiling and saying, 'You trusted me and I ended up defanging the snake. I did it. I did that', while Spencer smiles and says, 'Yeah, you did that, you did'. Approval for the sidekick, but thanks from Martha only go to Spencer, again centring him as the hero.

Being a zoologist is an interesting choice for this character, especially given the picaninny's closeness to animals of all sorts, as said earlier. He himself is called 'Mouse', and his affinity with animals is also shown when his name allows him to ride the elephant towards the end of the movie to enable the group to put the jewel back in the jaguar's eye and end the game. He is darker skinned, has a slight body, shorts, vest with his name on it, bandana necktie, rucksack and hat with turned back brim. In the bazaar, Fridge eats pound cake by mistake because Bethany mistook it for bread. He panics, 'Am I shaking? Am I breaking out? Am I still Black?' Then he explodes. That is clearly the punchline. Another exploding Black man as the joke, much like Terry Crews with the exploding/removed head/brain in Old Spice Power advertisements (Figure 4.4).

The Old Spice ads have something of a following on YouTube. They are reposted many times, often as compilations, such as 'Best Old Spice Commercials of All Time' from March 2021. Whether as compilations or not, what is striking

Figure 4.4 Actor Terry Crews poses shirtless for photographers on the floor of the New York Stock Exchange, August 19, 2010, Reuters/Alamy.

about these ads is that both Crews and Mustafa are naked from the waist up. They are not nudes but naked, meaning that they are available for pornographic consumption. The ads deal with the danger of the possibility of desire for the Black male body through making them the willing butt of the joke, through Black men's blackface humour. Terry Crews has an extremely defined, muscular, darker-skinned body in comparison to Mustafa's defined torso and arms, and wears shorts as opposed to Mustafa's jeans/trousers. In contrast, LL Cool J in Old Spice Swagger is fully clothed, as are the white men in other Old Spice ads. LL Cool J's Swagger ad is also without a hint of anti-Black man comedy. This example shows that Black men's blackface humour is clearly not necessary to sell Old Spice.

In the 2021 compilation, Terry Crews rides on a (stuffed) tiger's back. Why the tiger? We could say it is to show his link to the jungle and animality, except of course that tigers are not in the African continent, but jungles exist where tigers roam in India, for example. The fact of tigers' non-existence on the African continent does not matter in racist humour neither does the fact that the tiger is in fact a stuffed toy. This perhaps makes it more humorous to those who find it funny as he is playing into the stereotype of the black man, but one who stupidly has to resort to riding stuffed jungle cats. He is also in an ad where his head blows off. Unbelievably, the humour here is the head blowing off. The 'Black man's head severed from his body' joke is also present in the Old Spice 'Power' ad. Here Crews advertises power in a can, catches his own head and puts it back on. In 'Terry Crews' Greatest Hits' posted by the Old Spice Collaboration Team in 2019, Crews appears naked only wearing his signature shorts and very developed muscles, googly-eyed, mouth open. After saying his lines, 'It can block BO for 16 hours', his open-mouthed, googly-eyed head floats off. He then wakes up and says, 'I just had the worse dream'. We even see Crews' brain jetting off out of this cranium. The representation of Terry Crews' head blowing up, floating away, being put back on the body, or his brain jetting off out of his cranium, seems to me to be a ritual lynching of the hypermasculine black male body.

Supposed comedy anaesthetizes the 21st-century audience to past and present anti-Black man violence. It presents the chokehold as a comedy in which the part played by the black man is the muscular simpleton who can be disposed of by erasing his humanity through making him into a buffoon prior to his ritual lynching. The beheading is the punchline, the source of anti-Black man racist entertainment. Even though the muscular body is within view, this is no Black superhero then like 'the Falcon gliding across an urban skyline [which] symbolized the unprecedented access and upward social mobility many African Americans were experiencing in education and professional positions in the wake of hard-earned antidiscrimination laws and affirmative action' (Nama, 2011: 2). Rather, the Old Spice ads with Crews and Mustafa (Figure 4.5) take Black men back to the plantation.

Mustafa's most famous Old Spice words are arguably 'Be a man, man' and 'Ladies' while he does something ridiculous such as riding a horse backwards. The joke is on him with the smooth beautiful baritone voice, quirk of the eyebrows and hackneyed phrases of a Black seducer long feared in the plantation US and beyond as the sambo/coon dandy (Tate, 2020a). Body stands in for penis whose threat to whiteness is dealt with psychically through humour, with Mustafa as the butt of the joke. He seems to think he is cool, but he is racially branded as that white projection, Symbolic sambo (Wynter, 1979).

The Black man's naked torso continues to be fetish object in Mustafa's Old Spice ads. This links to what I said earlier in the discussion of *Lovecraft Country* that the torso exudes the white supposition of Black male vitality of skin, muscle and organs. Mustafa is a lighter-skin shade than Crews and much less muscular. Still, his body is fetish object where his chest stands in for his genitals, even while his slightly lighter skin tone makes him 'more feminine and thus less of a threat within the framework of Black masculinity' (Potts and Johnson, 2020: 91). So when he says, 'Be a man, man', he can only speak to other feminized

Figure 4.5 Old Spice nemeses Fabio and Isaiah Mustafa appear for a
special promotional appearance at the Grove Los Angeles,
California, WENN Rights Ltd/Alamy.

men like himself and his, 'Ladies', lacks heterosexual, hypersexual, seductive power. In the ads, both Crews and Mustafa are
caught in the panopticon (Foucault, 1975) of the white projection of the hypermasculine 'Mandingo' and assumption of
Black straight hypersexuality. This means they had to be seen to
be controllable/controlled by consumers in order to be commodities with skin value, much as was the case in enslavement.

Crews and Mustafa cannot wear their skin as they choose
and as a critique of the anti–Black world that they inhabit. That
is not the role of the skins of Black men wearing blackface.
Rather, the white gaze of dissection inhabits their skins. George
Yancy (2008) in *Black Bodies White Gazes* drawing on Fanon's
work writes about how Black bodies can disturb 'the tranquillity

of white life'. To forestall disturbance, Crews and Mustafa come into view in the ads as the known black man comedian through the erasure of Black men's humanity in the recycling of anti-Black male stereotypes. This then enables a return to white supremacist psychic, social, affective and political equilibrium. Old Spice ads do not return agency to Black men by deconstructing and decolonizing these stereotypes but continue to make Black men's bodies white possessions through humour. Black men's bodies as white possessions also remain in Black male *passing* and *being passed* as white in film and television.

Black whiteface in film and television: Passing and being passed in *The Human Stain* and *Prison Break*

Lola Young (Baroness Young of Hornsey) (1996) in looking at race and representation in British cinema states that as analysts we must trace coloniality, rather than only looking at negative or positive images. Further, we should look at the racialization of gender and sexuality in cinema as we discuss history and colonial discourse so that we can see how histories continue to be repeated, enacted and ceaselessly permeate cultural production. For Young, films are part of a complex matrix of ideas, fantasies and unconscious desires, anxieties and fears within politico-social and historical conjunctures. One of those fears is of Black passing for/as white as a calculated attempt to deceive and upend whiteness which must be outed and punished:

> The 'passing narrative often works in the service of preserving systems of inequality as opposed to dismantling them. A successful pass depends on the maintenance of binary identity categories and the existing hegemonic order, a fact that reinforces systems of inequality even as it aims to undermine them'
>
> (Kuryloski, 2019: 29–30)

Young (1996) states that actors who were known to be white played 'tragic' mixed-race protagonists in Hollywood passing films in the 1940s and 1950s. This casting underlies the idea that white audiences would not identify with Black actors in these lead roles. An exception to this casting practice appeared in the 1930s in light-skinned, white-appearing Fredi Washington. She was passed as white by her producers in order to make her palatable to white audiences who reacted to her as white until her Blackness was revealed, even though in her off-screen life, Washington refused to pass as white (Regester, 2010). She was cast as a 'white Negro' to play very light-skinned Peola Johnson in the film *Imitation of Life* (1934 released in 1936, Director John M. Stahl, Universal Pictures, based on Fannie Hurst's novel of the same title, and remade in 1959 by Douglas Sirk).

Peola was passing as white in 1930s US and rejects her own (Black) mother, Delilah Johnson (Louise Beavers), in order to separate herself from Blackness through her masquerade as white. In this racial masking, she uses the visible marker of that racial claim, her light skin and her short-lived marriage to a white man (Regester, 2010). In the book, Peola also ensures that the mask of skin cannot be lifted when she gets sterilized so that no future children will reveal her Blackness. Like Washington, in his off-screen life, Wentworth Miller asserts his Blackness. He has also played 'the tragic mulatto' part of a light-skinned Black man passing as white and rejecting his family in the process in *The Human Stain* and has been passed into whiteness in order for the part he played in *Prison Break* to be acceptable to and believable by white audiences.

UK-born Wentworth Miller is Black/white 'mixed race'. His father is of African American and Jamaican descent, already mixed categories because of enslavement histories, and his mother is white US American. He claims British and American citizenship, can claim Jamaican citizenship and at the time of his birth in Chipping Norton in the UK in 1972, he would have still been the nation's problem 'half-caste'. At birth, his Black/white 'mixed-race' body provided a psychic and skin border to whiteness connected to centuries of anti-African descent racism and now to 21st-century neoliberal 'post-race' racialization alongside continuing Black-phobia. The intensity of fear/hate surrounding racialized body bordering should make it impossible for him to be read as white. His passing in film and being *passed* on television as white emphasizes that whiteness is more than skin colour, but skin's *recognition* as white dictates who can transform dispossession in historical 'half-caste/mulatto' segregation and 'post-race' US/UK. To develop this argument on the libidinal economy of fear/hate and Black male passing, the discussion first turns to mixing as a US/UK problem and opportunity before looking at passing in *The Human Stain* that highlights white possession of body, psyche and life. The analysis also looks at what recognition of him as a Black/white 'mixed-race' man being *passed as* white does in that moment through analysis of both the film and *Prison Break*. Last, it focuses on whiteness and Black/white 'mixed-race' dispossession in 21st-century, 'post-race' US/UK.

The US's 'tragic mulatto' stereotype means that cinema and television strategies reproduce the colonial ontological status of Black/white 'mixed-race' people only in terms of aliena-tion, dishonour, violence and non-whiteness. The only gram-mar through which race mixing has been known is deficit, psychological dysfunction and societal marginalization. As a 'tragic mulatto', Miller's body exists within a 'libidinal econ-omy' related to political economy, (hetero) sexuality and the unconscious (Wilderson 111, 2010: 7). Film and television continue to construct the 'tragic mulatto' body as a patholog-ical site of perpetual suffering because of 'race mixing'. The 'tragic mulatto' is a fetish object of white 'racial' hygiene in colonial and contemporary times. The colonial grammar of suffering ensures that (s)he becomes anti-human if the HuMan and human are always constructed as 'racially pure'. Appear-ing as a product of modernity, (s)he is a 'new race', societally marginal and the tragedy of un-belonging is their ontological condition.

White kinship within societies structured by racial domi-nance is no guarantee of being part of the white national body. In the US, for Naomi Zack (1993: 39–40), the 'proscriptive white kinship schema reinforces and perpetuates ordinary ideas about physical races as natural entities' rather than seeing that the 'white breeding schema of family identity is a form of social technology'. The social technology of the white breeding schema is another part of the race epistemologies of ignorance (Mills, 1997) that attempts to remain hidden to continue the lore of 'post-race' inclusivity. The 'tragic mulatto' as racial hygiene keeps this schema in place. This is even the case many decades past *Loving v Virginia's* (1967) ruling that inter-racial marriage was legal in all of the US because neither transracial intimacy nor Black/white 'mixed-racedness' has become normalized.

However, the multi-racial movement exists within a 21st-century liberal humanist discursive terrain of 'meritocracy', 'multiculturalism' and 'diversity'. Simultaneously, there is continuing anti-Black racism, as we see in '#Black Lives Matter' 2020 and #SayHerName. Anti-Blackness and 'diversity' co-exist within 'the strange enigma of race in contemporary America' which Eduardo Bonilla-Silva (2010) terms 'colour-blind racism'. In US 'colour-blind racism', Blacks and darker-skinned minorities lag behind whites in all spheres of social life, and colour-coded inequality relegates intersectional racial injustice to individual and/or cultural limitations rather than societal racial structuration and white supremacy. Black/white transracial intimacies are problematized, for example, because of 'the children' or the extra emotional burden on couples, maintaining the racial order of mono-racial intimacy while whites now claim to be victims of 'reverse racism' (Bonilla-Silva, 2010). This is part of the Black/white 'mixed-race' socio-political terrain of US 'colour-blind racism'.

Black/white transracial intimacy has a long history of national and governmental problematization in the UK. Mark Christian's (2008) analysis of the Fletcher Report (1930)[1] is an illustration of this. This report was eugenicist in tone and constructed Black/white, what it called 'half-caste', children as 'genetically abnormal'. It described their transracial families as poverty-ridden and immoral. The report's legacy was moral panic and stereotyping of the Black/white 'mixed-race' population. The white British fear-hate of 'half-caste children' in the heart of the Empire after World War II prompted more moral panic because of the mixing of mobilized white British women and Black colonial mobilized men (Carby, 2007). In fact, in 1942, the Colonial Office's anxiety about the future of the UK population arose from what it saw as the sexual invasion of Black soldiers (Carby, 2007). After the war, by 1947, Black/white 'mixed-race' orphans became the nation's 'lonely picaninny' (Carby, 2007), and in the 1950s, the colonial extra-legal anti-miscegenation regime (Thompson, 2009) was transformed into the 'colour bar' in public spaces. The 'colour bar' aimed to minimize heterosexual transracial intimacy.

Public governmental problematization of 'mixed-race' bodies in the UK continued in 2006. Trevor Phillips OBE[2], then chair of the now defunct Commission for Racial Equality, highlighted 'mixed-race' pathology in a report made to Tony Blair's Labour government. He described this pathology as 'more than average' familial and individual dysfunction – lone parenthood, family breakdown, drug treatment and identity stripping because 'mixed-race' people are 'marooned between communities'. Paradoxically, white kinship marked on Black/white 'mixed-race' skin is advantageous within 'chromato-cratic' UK/US societies even though 'the tragic mulatto' speaks anxiety, fear and trauma, as we see in Fletcher, Phillips and Miller in *The Human Stain*.

In the UK, there is an emerging 21st-century utopian view that 'mixed-race' people are the new faces of a multicultural nation. For example, Dame Jessica Ennis-Hill's global iconicity as skin representative of the nation for the London 2012 Olympic Games and the aesthetic, political, social and economic value produced by her lighter-skinned Black/white 'mixed-race' body for the nation (Tate, 2016a). The UK's 21st-century skin politics is one in which the acceptable face of Blackness is only a visibly Black/white 'mixed-race' one. We also see this across the Atlantic in the skin of the late Miss USA 2019 Cheslie Kryst (April 28, 1991–January 30, 2021; Figure 4.6). This new 'mulatticity' (Carr, 2002) is linked to colonialism and enslavement's 'chromatocracy'. However, it is a fantasy that Black/white 'mixed-race' skin value indicates racism's demise in the UK/US and the emergence of racial equality.

Figure 4.6 Cheslie Kryst NHL Awards, Las Vegas, June 19, 2019, Everett Collection Inc/Alamy.

Irrespective of these exceptions, in post-Brexit Britain and post-Trump US, the body politics of the Racial Contract's libidinal economy ensures white hegemony because:

> [...] globally and within particular nations [...] white people, Europeans and their descendants, continue to benefit from the Racial Contract, which creates a world in their cultural image, political states differentially favouring their interests, an economy structured around the racial exploitation of others, and a moral psychology (not just in whites sometimes in non-whites also), skewed consciously and unconsciously toward privileging them, taking the status quo of differential racial entitlement as normatively legitimate, and not to be investigated further.
>
> (Mills, 1997: 40)

The Racial Contract constructs a white world through an epistemology of ignorance, 'a particular pattern of localized and global cognitive dysfunctions' that function psychologically and socially 'producing the ironic outcome that whites will in general be unable to understand the world they themselves have made' (Mills, 1997: 18). That is, there can be a turn to 'white innocence' (Wekker, 2016) whenever a charge of racism is made. Therefore, ignorance is not an unknowing, an absence of knowledge about. Ignorance is a *will to silence* (Foucault, 1980) knowledge of white privilege, anti-Black racism and 'colour-blind' ideology. This produces 'unknowledges' which 'sometimes […] are consciously generated, while at other times they are unconsciously generated and supported […] [but] they work to support white privilege and supremacy' (Sullivan and Tuana, 2007: 1–2). Unknowledges undergird colonial skin governance through state and societal processes, structures, knowledge and affects even whilst Black/white 'mixed-race' bodies have 21st-century, 'post-race' skin value for the nation as a sign of its racial tolerance.

However, within national (in)tolerance of 'mixing', Black/white 'mixed-race' problematization is carried through anti-Black racism's affects – disgust, contempt, hate, anxiety, fear, shame, fascination. 'The (un)tolerated' are 'perceived to be harmless or relatively unthreatening' as recognized mechanisms for dissent and change (Ngai, 2005), and racism is now constructed as only the actions of a few rogue white right-wing individuals at the fringes of normative politics. However, racism is at the very heart of UK/US skin politics. Skin's colonial politics generates a racial epidermal schema (Fanon, 2021) so that Black/white 'mixed-race' people experience racism's negative affects because of 'race mixing', even whilst paradoxically 'race mixing' is taken societally as an illustration of racial tolerance. As was the case in colonialism, libidinal economies within anti-miscegenation regimes speak of 'proper' white sexuality and family life as an obligation for citizenship (Stoler, 1995, 2002). Black/white 'mixed-race' dysfunction, the 'tragic mulatto' and 'lonely picaninny' are discursive constructs of white racial hygiene. That is, they are focused on keeping the white race 'pure'. Black/white 'mixed-race' bodies are placed outside of the *nation as white family* because of anti-Black racism and national intolerance (Elam, 2011) while providing the terrain for the nation's claim to tolerance, civilization and modernity itself (Lewis, 2005).

We can see this 'being kept outside of the nation as white family' in hypo-descent. Hypo-descent, 'the one-drop rule', means that Black ancestry makes one Black irrespective of lightness of skin, as we saw in the case of Fredi Washington earlier in the chapter (Ali, 2003; Ifekwunigwe, 1999; Olumide, 2002; Russell et al., 1992; Zack, 1993). This mark of 'race' still continues even though post-structuralist and decolonial thinking has shown us that identity is shifting, never fixed in a once-and-for-all way (Hall, 1996a, b); 'race' is a social construct (Ifekwunigwe, 1999); culture is hybrid (Bhabha, 1990); and, racialized identifications are performative (Tate, 2005). Black/white 'mixed-race' subjects cannot represent national values as the heteronormative family, and its gendered practices are already scripted as white and Christian, establishing the standards to which the nation's racialized others should or must aspire (Lewis, 2005). A racialized libidinal economy in majority white countries keeps the nation white. This shows that transracial intimacy is more than about the affect love. It is also about white racial biopolitical power as it maintains white racial dominance, disciplines bodies and manages life. Anti-Black racism is still embedded within heterosexual intimacy because 'the inferior other becomes a fundamental project for the establishment of the superior self whose superiority is a function of what it *is*' (Gordon, 1997: 70). Let us now move to thinking through some of this discussion through film and television.

The Human Stain (2003, Director Robert Benton; Screenplay Nicholas Meyer) is based on the novel of the same name by Philip Roth (2000):

> Philip Roth's is perhaps one of richest and most unusual meditations on crossing racial and cultural boundaries in twenty-first-century American fiction. In it we find the

author, Philip Roth, imagining a Jewish character, Nathan Zuckerman, with an autobiography similar to that of Roth himself, with Zuckerman, in turn, imagining an African American character, Coleman Silk, who is "passing" as a white Jew.

(Elliott, 2020: 92)

The film begins with Coleman Silk's (Anthony Hopkins) and his lover Faunia Farley's (Nicole Kidman) deaths when they are forced off the road into an icy river by her ex-husband Lester Farley's (Ed Harris) car. From that point on, Coleman's story of passing is revealed in a series of scenes intermingled with his past and current life. Nearly 18 years old, Coleman (Wentworth Miller) is from a Black middle-class family. He is a valedictorian at East Orange High School with a 4.0 GPA and an amateur boxer. His boxing coach wants him to have a match to show an athletics recruiter from Pitt how good he is. He thinks his boxing skills, added to the fact that he is a valedictorian, should get him an athletics scholarship. Coleman says his father expects him to go to Howard. His coach then begins his life of passing by saying, 'One thing, when you meet the guy from Pitt, don't tell him you're coloured, okay?' Coleman looks astonished, 'Don't tell him?' His coach says, 'Don't bring it up. You're neither one thing or the other. You're Silky Silk that's all'. Coleman asks, 'He won't know?' His coach says that Coleman is the top kid from East Orange High, and 'he'll think you're Jewish'. Jewish whiteness replaces Black, 'neither-one-thing-or-the-other' made possible through his light skin (and straighter hair). His white coach sets out for him the extreme individualism and alienation of passing for white that he chooses to live his whole life. He must cast himself adrift from the moorings of his Black family and identity to find himself as white throughout a life of negating his Blackness. He lives though with the perpetual fear of white discovery and white hate. We see this casting adrift also in his choice not to go to Howard, a Historically Black University.

His mother (Anna Deavere Smith) is a nurse. His father (Harry Lennix) lost his optician's business in the depression and worked with the railway as a waiter in the restaurant car until his death at work. He lives with his parents, sister Ernestine (Marie Michel) and brother Walter (Danny Blanco Hall). His father expects him to go to Howard like his brother and then on to become a doctor if that is what he wants to do. His father retires him from boxing before he dies on the job in the dining car on a train. On the day of his father's Black Christian funeral, his mother is heading to work, and Coleman tells her he did not really know what his father went through daily. He says, 'The point is if you're coloured, it doesn't matter how much you know. You'll work in the dining car'. Coleman rightly fears anti-Black racism and the impact of white hate on his social mobility. He does not want to be the white world's 'Negro'.

His mother tells him that his father worked in the dining car so he would not have to, and his father's insurance and his academic record will get Coleman into Howard. Coleman responds, 'I heard about Howard from Walt. They are always talking about the Negro people, about we the Negro people. I am not a political person, Mom. I don't understand what we is'. His mother asks him, 'Who do you think you are?' And Coleman replies, 'I know who I am'. His mother tells him, 'You need to be proud of your race'. Coleman's next response shows that he refuses to be the Black community's Negro as well as his declaration that as non-political he does not know what 'we' is. He is an individual, 'What about me? What about being proud of just being me, it's my life or don't I get any say in the matter?' He refuses to go to Howard and instead is drafted into the Navy as white with hazel eyes, the descriptions of himself he selected on the registration form. Here begins his life as a white Jewish man not the white or Black 'Negro' that he has utterly repudiated.

We also see this repudiation in his romantic relationships and in his short boxing career. In the St Nicholas Arena fight, 162 pounds Silky Silk fights 170 pounds Sugar Pete Cunningham (Peter Cunningham), a darker-skinned Black boxer. His coach advises him to put on a show for the audience but Coleman mercilessly beats Sugar Pete to a bloody pulp and wins in the first round. This extreme, cruel beating makes us wonder about its exact nature. Could this be Coleman trying so hard to distance himself from Blackness that he had to become this Black man's terror so that he could be unmistakably white? In front of his Black darker-skinned corner man (Neville Edwards), a nameless character in the film, his coach berates him for not giving people their money's worth. Coleman retorts angrily, 'What, I'm supposed to let him hit me in the head 5, 10 times to put on a show? I ain't holding up no nigger'. His corner man says nothing as the camera shot focuses on him, who Coleman makes 'a nigger', marking him as both the cause and the victim of white offence in order to conceal that he is also 'a nigger'.

Concealment of Blackness and living as a white Jewish man extends into his love life. While a student at New York University (NYU), he used 'to go to the library stacks and come out with girls', as he tells his friend Nathan Zuckerman (Gary Sinise). He meets and falls in love with white, blond, Scandinavian Mid-West US descent Steena Paulsson (Jacinda Barrett), who thinks he is Jewish American. She is the woman who retired Classics Professor Coleman (Anthony Hopkins) tells Nathan that he nearly married. Steena and Coleman go to see his mother in New Jersey one Sunday and Steena hopes that his mother will like her. Coleman's mother opens the door to his knock. He kisses her on the cheek and introduces her to Steena as his mother. During dinner, Steena speaks non-stop about her Scandinavian family and refuses to hold hands with Coleman. On the train, going back to New York, Steena is visibly upset, won't make eye contact and crying, tells Coleman, 'I can't do this, Coleman, I love you but I can't'. She leaves him looking shocked on the train. He learned racial concealment from this experience of love not conquering race hate, so when he meets Iris (Mili Avital), his white Jewish passing continues and his Black erasure deepens.

He shows a picture of Iris to his mother and tells her they will get married in June. His mother asks if he has told her or if he will tell her and is he planning to bring her home for dinner. He shocks his mother by telling her that he told Iris that his parents are dead. He denies the existence of his mother and siblings Ernestine and Walter because 'I don't want to be Coleman Silk, the Negro Classics Professor and that is how it would always come out, Mom. You know it and I know it'. He justifies his passing by critiquing the US race hierarchy of the one-drop rule through which he does not want to be victimized. His mother responds, 'Funny, I never thought of you as Black or white. Gold. You were my golden child'. This is an interesting commentary given that the family is proud of their Blackness. She is here being critical of the very system that Coleman rails against for not seeing him as an individual. In this statement, she is reaching for a 'post-race' utopia that does not exist. You cannot be neither-one-thing-or-the-other because of the colonial historico-racial schema and the white gaze of dissection carried within the one-drop rule.

She asks if Coleman will ever tell Iris, and his evasive answer leads her to a tense monologue as Coleman listens silently to her possible future, where she will never see her grandchildren except at Penn Station on a prearranged Sunday morning as they pass by. She predicts that will be her birthday present five years into the future, but she would be there to silently watch them pass by. She continues, 'But aren't you taking a risk having children? The suspense will be unbearable. Suppose they don't pop out of her womb as white as you, won't you have some explaining to do? Will you accuse her of adultery with a Negro?' Coleman looks tense and without an answer to her warnings about him passing, he says he has to go. His mother responds, 'Coleman you think like a prisoner. You are white as snow yet you think like a slave'. The freedom of passing for white through skin does not translate into liberation. Coleman is still a prisoner of white supremacist race thinking's fear and hate because he will not accept his Blackness. In his passing, he seems to feel no guilt or anxiety as he renounces his past, erasing his Black family in order to succeed in the system of US racial hierarchy by passing as white Jewish.

In 1998, at the time of President Clinton's impeachment following the Monica Lewinski affair, we see Coleman (Anthony

Hopkins) a Classics professor and powerful college dean at the mainly white Athena College in West Massachusetts. Educated at NYU and Oxford University, and after having taught in England, Coleman returned to the US as one of the first Jews to teach in a Classics Department anywhere in the US. He made Athena excellent but made enemies on the way. In a class he is teaching, he mentions that he has not seen two students for the entire semester and asks the class if anyone knows if they are 'real students or are they spooks?' The absent students William Thomas and Tracy Cummings are both African Americans and, Tracy, who was devastated, makes a complaint about the racist slur. In the adversarial disciplinary hearing chaired by Professor Delphine Roux (Mimi Kuzyk), Coleman says he did not know they were African American because he has never seen them, and his use of spooks was not racist, but he was using the dictionary definition of 'ghost, spectre'. When reminded that the second definition in the dictionary was 'derogatory, negro', he responds that he had 'never laid eyes on them. How could I know they were Black? All I did know is that they were invisible'. He continues, '[T]hese students have never attended a single class, do they exist or are they spooks? Consider the context. So Ms Cummings is devastated is she? Give me a break. To charge me with racism is not only false, it is spectacularly false and you know it'. As he leaves the room, he slaps the back of Herb Keble (Ron Canada) in a sarcastic thank you. He had appointed Herb as the first African American ever on the campus when he was dean. Herb had refused to help and remained silent throughout the proceedings. To continue to be able to live as a white man, he must accept the vilification of his peers on the disciplinary committee because he perpetrated anti-Black racism through the slur 'spooks'. At home, he rages, telling his wife Iris (Phyllis Newman) that he has resigned. However, as they plan what legal action to take, she dies. She dies without knowing that Coleman is Black. They appear to be childless. Perhaps Coleman could not take the risk of discovery of his passing for white as his mother had warned him?

His last love interest is Faunia Farley with whom he dies as said earlier. Faunia is dysfunctional, psychologically damaged, white, works three part-time, low-paid jobs at the post office, a dairy farm and as a janitor at the college. She is much younger than Coleman, and life has dealt her many blows. She was born into a wealthy family, but her parents got divorced, and her new stepfather sexually abused her, penetrating her with his fingers while he read her stories at bedtime. When he tried to have sex with her at 14, she left for Florida after her mother had not believed her about the abuse for years. She lost contact with her mother. Her two children with her ex-husband Lester Farley (Ed Harris) died from smoke inhalation because of a faulty heater, but she survived because of the firefighters. She carries their ashes with her and does not know if she should keep them or bury them. Lester is a war veteran, psychotic, abusive, stalks her constantly and drives them off the road to their deaths because he wanted to kill 'the Jew'.

At Coleman's Jewish funeral, Nathan Zuckerman realizes that his friend is Black when he meets Ernestine (Lizan Mitchell). Coleman was still sending Ernestine birthday cards, so they seemed to have remained in contact, but Walter shunned him when his mother was still alive saying he never wanted to see his 'lily white face' again. Ernestine says to Nathan Zuckerman after Coleman's funeral that it was, 'sad that Coleman felt he had to construct his whole life around a lie. Coleman could have stopped that racism charge in its tracks if he had just told the truth'. Zuckerman responds, 'But that is the one thing he couldn't do'. The only person he told was Faunia. Why, one wonders? Was it because his academic life was over so it no longer mattered? Was it because he could not carry the burden of his passing any longer? Was it because he wanted to show Faunia his racial flaw, his human stain of Blackness so that she could finally accept herself, him as a middle-class, educated man and them as an intimate couple? Was it because if Faunia ever told the secret, then it was deniable because of his eminent life lived as a white Jewish academic and his class position as opposed to her 'trailer trash life' as she calls it? We will never know. What is clear is that race fear – his own of being 'the

Negro' and of discovery of his passing as white Jewish, Steena's of Black pollution – and hate – his refusal to be proud of his race rather than just himself and Lester's (and likely some of his colleagues') anti-Semitism – dictated how he felt he could live his life. As his mother said, he was a slave. He lived his life as a slave to white supremacist race skin diktats. He remained a white possession because of his passing as white. Of course, what he also showed is that whiteness is skin deep; race is performative not fixed in biology; skin still dictates who has power and privilege and who is destined to die on the job in a train dining car.

The runaway hit *Prison Break* (Director Paul Scheuring, FOX; Figure 4.7) ran simultaneously for five seasons (2005–2017), on US and UK television. Using an escape plan tattooed onto his body, the lead character Michael Scofield (Wentworth Miller) saves innocent brother Lincoln Burrows (Dominic Purcell) from the electric chair by breaking out of Fox River Penitentiary along with other inmates. Michael's love interest Sara Tancredi (Sarah Wayne Callies) the prison doctor, helps

Figure 4.7 Beverly Hills, California, USA, March 29, 2017, *Prison Break* cast, Dominic Purcel (right), Wentworth Miller (2nd from right) at the Paley Center for Media.

them. Michael is the mastermind from the beginning to take down 'The Company' which is the only way for them all to be free.

In this series, we see no mention of Michael as Black/white 'mixed race' even though as the audience we know that about him in his off-screen life. The series refused to foreground race as a source of obvious contestation even whilst the breakout team is Black, Hispanic and white. Miller became white on the small screen. What does Black/white 'mixed-race' Miller as lead protagonist being *passed as* white mean for skin politics within 'post-race' racial skin dissection? This question is an important one. This is so as what we are seeing in the case of race erasure within the series is that, '[…] Civil society represents itself to itself as being infinitely inclusive, and its technologies of hegemony (including cinema) are mobilized to manufacture this assertion not to dissent from it' (Wilderson 111, 2010: 24). Indeed, films [and, in this case, television series] 'can be thought of as one of an ensemble of discursive practices mobilized by civil society to invite, or interpellate, Blacks to the same variety of social identities that other races are able to embody without contradiction' (Wilderson 111, 2010: 24). However, what we see in *Prison Break* is an active whitening of the lead character through requiring the audience suspension of belief in terms of his racialized off-screen reality and Black/white 'mixed-race' body. There is no invitation or interpellation of Blacks here but erasure and the continuing expectation that the lead protagonist and the 'prison break mastermind' can only be white. Civil society remains only inclusive of whiteness irrespective of the mobilization of its technologies of hegemony. This remains the case because of the epistemologies of ignorance (Mills, 1997, 2007) of the tragic mulatto stereotype. Given all of this, what (mis)recognition does Miller *being passed as white* in *Prison Break* instantiate, and why was this necessary?

Frantz Fanon (2021) inserts a decolonizing analysis of the coloniality of power, being, knowledge and affect into Merleau Ponty's deracinated reflections on corporeal schema. He does this by discussing racism's hold on colonial Black and white psyches. Fanon's historico-racial schema highlight white colonial

discourses on racial difference, racial structuration and institutionalization of white racial dominance, cultural consciousness, social practices and knowledge production. We become
ourselves in the eyes of others as they recognize us through a
racialized process. Drawing on Fanon's work, George Yancy
(2012: 152) speaks about the dissection of the white gaze that
'renders the black body ontologically truncated, fixed like an
essence'. Racial dissection operates as 'a form of bodily fragmentation, "visual mutilation" and reduction' (Yancy, 2012:
153). Transracial intimacy and Black/white 'mixed-race' subjects are caught within the intersectional matrix of dissection's
racialized recognition because:

> the autological subject, the genealogical society, their
> modes of intimacy and their material anchors emerged
> from European Empire as a mode and maneuver of
> domination and exploitation and continue to operate as
> such. [...Thus] the intimate couple is a key transfer point
> between, on the one hand, liberal imaginaries of contrac-
> tual economics, politics and sociality and on the other
> liberal forms of power in the contemporary world. [...]
> If the intimate couple is a key transfer point within lib-
> eralism this couple is already conditioned by liberalism's
> emergence and dispersion in empire.
>
> (Povinelli, 2006: 16)

Liberalism, still resonating with empire's anti-Black racism
and Black/white 'mixed-race' politics speaks to 'colour-blind'
racism, 'post-race' claims and 'mixed-race' body values. Even
though Miller is *passed as white* in *Prison Break* and his body
comes to *speak for and to* all whites, empire politics persist.
Passed as white is different from *passing for* white as it relates to a
different racialized scopic regime. It is a racial dissection *looking
over while overlooking* racial difference, an 'envisaging' (Derrida,
2005) wilfully refusing otherness from whiteness.

As Sara Ahmed (1999: 87) reminds us, '[T]he subject is
never what they image themselves to be nor are they simply
self-evidently there'. *Everyone passes.* As Miller in *The Human*

Stain shows, racial passing is not transgressive but makes individual sense in response to racialized social antagonism. However, passing as white or as Black does matter politically, and Miller in his off-screen life refuses to pass as white. Miller lives his life as a gay, Black/white, 'mixed-race' man who speaks about the overt racism he experiences irrespective of his celebrity, whilst as an actor his body is *being passed as* white. This *being passing as* resists the racialized scopic regime of essential difference and the disturbance supposedly 'racially ambiguous' bodies cause to coloniality's knowledge/power/being/affect. With each disturbance by such bodies, whiteness resurfaces as differences, and ambiguities are re-incorporated. In film and television, *being passed as* white can momentarily alter racial difference's systematization but always pauses on the visual cues of white skin. As self-imagined unmarked norm, whiteness fixates on Miller's racial ambiguity, ensuring that 'acts of passing become mechanisms for the recreation of [white] nation space' (Ahmed, 1999: 93).

Miller as white establishes a *'third space'* (Bhabha, 1990) or *'critical thirding'* (Soja, 1996), attempting to move past racial binaries but held fast by them. This is so as new white subject positions emerge through race performativity (Tate, 2005) even if only for a moment. The empathetic identification of the audience with Black/white 'mixed-race' Miller-as-white-Michael Schofield destabilizes whiteness as a structure of domination and location of affective attachment. Paradoxically, empathetic identification also produces racial domination. Empathetic identification is part of the process where 'blackness provided the occasion for [white] self-reflection as well as for an exploration of terror, desire, fear, loathing and longing [...] the role of feelings in securing domination [is important in the] obliteration of the other through the slipping on of blackness' (Hartman, 1997: 7). We saw this earlier in the discussion of the libidinal economy of white and black blackface.

However, what about the role of affect in securing domination in the obliteration of Blackness through the slipping on of whiteness? *Being passed as white* only works because the national audience gets something back. Miller is located within the national US/UK 'post-race' libidinal economy where his skin bridges Black and white consumers because of the social, economic and cultural capitals of skin colour, class and celebrity. His lighter-skinned Black/white, 'mixed-race' body extends to white bodies through the route of recognition so that 'post-racial' white guilt and shame because of racism transforms to white pleasure because of white tolerance (Tate, 2015a). The white audience then becomes innocent of racism (Wekker, 2016) because they have *passed him as* white. Miller's skin is a fetish object. His skin stands in for all Black/white 'mixed-race' people. His skin is the fungible (Hartman, 1997) organic matter which maintains white domination because 'race mixedness' is tangible proof of US/ UK tolerance. His skin remains caught, valuable within this 'post-race' libidinal economy, and his possession by whiteness is complete even as a celebrity.

Whilst in the 21st century, celebrity is more racially democratic, fame is racially ordered. Adulation, identification with and emulation of the famous are key elements in celebrity culture (Holmes and Redmond, 2006). Fame gives Miller's skin material, social, cultural, affective and psychic value because we desire fame, stars, celebrities, so as fans, we celebrate the famous and co-create their fame through fandom (Holmes and Redmond, 2006). White fans reach out for Miller to engage in a self-directed healing process based on developing 'intimacy' with him. Miller's skin becomes a site of pleasure. It produces cannibalistic affective attachment as fans pass through it to re-make themselves. Attachment to (real-life) Black/white 'mixed-race' corporeality remade acceptably white on television through race erasure highlights the social, political, cultural, affective and psychic value of his skin for white identification which in turn leads to their passing as 'post-race'. That is, where the post in 'post-race' is literally taken to mean that we are now beyond race; race is long dead; race no longer matters; racism does not exist, and we all live neoliberal lives. His skin produces a matrix of corporeality, power, gender, 'race', class, (hetero)sexuality and celebrity that speaks back to our very imaginings of him as 'white'.

There is white pleasure to be had through his *passed as white* skin, through 'catachresis' (Spivak, 1990). That is, the act of reversing, displacing, grasping and transforming the value coding apparatus. However, Miller's *being passed as white* on screen does not transform the racial value coding apparatus of 'race' but shows whose skin can extend to whiteness. That is, only one that has a white surface appearance, one that *looks* white. Miller's passing has a positive outcome for the white self and nation as it enables catharsis. Here, I mean, the emotional discharge of white racist shame produced by the empathetic identification with the skin of the Black-white 'mixed-race' man as those racialized as white pass through it. This is a peculiar 'race' performativity of 'the opposite'. Envisaged as non-threatening after *being passed*, Miller is avidly consumed through white affects, such as pleasure, shame, guilt, empathy and love.

Conclusion

This chapter has looked at skin colour politics as it relates to the libidinal economies that surround Black men's bodies by looking at the chokehold as part of representations. The analysis has unpacked the affects attached to Black men's skin as a continuation from colonial times to contemporary coloniality within representations of Black men in films, television and advertising. It has meditated on representation in advertising, film and television, reading the colonial tropes' continuities in the controlling images within representations of Black men as sambo, hypersexual, comedians, hypermasculine, perpetually infantile, aggressive, for example. The analysis used the trope of blackface in its white and black incarnations to unpick the violence of white hate, fear, desire and fetishization meted out to Black men through these representations. It highlighted the continuing centrality of the visual in 20th- and 21st-century race regimes through looking at Black/white 'mixed-race' male passing for white and being passed as white in the work of Wentworth Miller. Looking at passing through the figure of the masculinized body unsettles the gender expectation of the tragic mulatto trope of the racial passer which is usually a woman like Peola in *Imitation of Life*. The white audience itself is allowed to pass through the body of Miller, enabling white liberal subjectivities to emerge through the consumption of empathetic attachment, producing affects such as love, shame, guilt. Chapter 5 continues to look at skin colour politics focusing on Black feminized bodies in global beauty pageants.

Notes

1 This report was researched and written by Muriel Fletcher between 1928 and 1930, supported by the Association for the Welfare of Half-Caste Children and the University of Liverpool. The Fletcher Report used the derogatory term 'half-caste' and embedded it into the social perception of Liverpool with its well-established Black community (by the end of World War 1). Further, 'Fletcher gave reasons for the dysfunctionality of "half caste" children caught in a union between Black and white parents as being due to the fusion of different outlooks and cultures' (Christian, 2008: 230). Fletcher stated, '[F]rankly [...] it is [...] the inferior hereditary and family structure, along with the low moral standards, of "half-caste" families that is the root of [the children's] socioeconomic poverty-stricken condition' (Christian, 2008: 234).

2 Most Excellent Order of the British Empire rewards contributions to the arts and sciences, and work with civil society organizations.

5 Beauty pageants

The global politics of skin shade

Introduction

Beauty pageants are national and global locations for struggles over skin colour politics, body shape preferences and the racialization of hair texture, as well as the interaction of global/local aesthetics and geopolitical power relations. At the local level, what Natasha Barnes (1994) calls 'the face of the nation' is a site of positive affective attachment by audiences in national imaginings of self and community which we can also extend to global beauty pageants. Throughout the 20th century, globally and locally light/white skin and straight/straighter hair texture have been the revered iconic ideal. However, 2019 was widely feted as the year in which there was a break in this pattern of the global politics of skin shade because the winners of five major pageants were Black. This chapter takes as its central problematic the question of this 'break' in light/white beauty iconicity to interrogate whether this means an end to colonial hate of Black skin in the 21st century or points to its continuation in the global consumption of lighter Black skin as signifier of 'post-race' anti-Black racism in the Global North-West and South-West. The chapter begins by analyzing the film *Misbehaviour* (March 12, 2020, Director Philippa Lowthorpe, 20th Century Studios, Screenplay Rebecca Frayn, Gaby Chiappe) to think through global skin colour politics and the geopolitical relationships between women based on colonial ideology. The film is a British comedy drama about a Women's

DOI: 10.4324/b23223-5

Liberation Movement (WLM) plan led by Sally Alexander (Keira Knightley) to disrupt the 1970 Miss World beauty pageant in London (won by Miss Grenada Jennifer Hosten, whose book on this pageant was the inspiration for the movie), within the backdrop of the protests of the anti-apartheid movement against South Africa being allowed to participate. This led to two contestants from that country being entered, white Miss South Africa (Jillian Jessup) and Black Miss Africa South (Pearl Jansen who was first runner-up). Nearly 50 years later, in 2019, five major beauty pageants were all won by Black women for the first time – Miss Universe (Zozibini Tunzi, South Africa), Miss World (Toni-Ann Singh, Jamaica, a country which has had three other winners), Miss America (Nia Franklin), Miss USA (the late Cheslie Kryst who died on January 30, 2022) and Miss Teen USA (Kaliegh Garris). Looking at the example of Jamaica's beauty politics and pageant winners, the chapter engages in a discussion of what a 'break' in white/lighter skin iconicity means for Black beauty futures in which features, skin shade and body shape maintain colonial beauty ideals which mask Black skins. Let us turn to look at a brief history of Black British feminism as a response to colonialism and coloniality and distinct from the British WLM, to provide a context for reading the film.

Coloniality and 'misbehaviour'

The use of the term 'Black' by Black British feminists evolved in the 1940s as an anti-colonial signifier forming political solidarities between African and Indian liberation activists seeking to counter British imperialism (Mirza, 2022). Heidi Safia Mirza (2022) charts Black British feminism but admits that its plotting cannot be linear, and it cannot be confined to the first, second and third waves of white British feminism. Rather, the Black British feminist genealogical project is about quilting memories of the past and present in order to get a coherent whole. Of course, this coherence can vary in terms of what Black British feminists and historians of Black British feminisms see as foundational publications, organizations and events. In the 1970s UK, Black, post-/anti-colonial and anti-racist feminists critiqued white feminism's limitations because of its racist exclusion of Black women's concerns, a masculinized antiracist movement and a multicultural discourse that did not incorporate an understanding of intersectionality (Mirza, 2022). In the 1980s, Black British feminism can be charted through landmark publications. Hazel Carby's (1982) intervention 'White Women Listen! Black Feminism and the Boundaries of Sisterhood' in *The Empire Strikes Back: Race and Racism in 70's Britain*, further defined Black British feminist activism and theory, setting it apart from Black feminism in the US. The Black Cultural Archives Black women's oral history project 'Heart of the Race' and the British Library's 'Sisterhood and After' project both document this history, along with the founding mothers of Black British feminism. There have been individual Black British feminists whose stories have also been told. Una Marson, who campaigned for the League of Coloured Peoples in the 1940s (Jarrett-Macauley, 2009); and Claudia Jones in the 1950s, who established the Notting Hill Carnival in London and Britain's first commercial Black newspaper, the *West Indian Gazette*. Jones also organized the first televised Black beauty competition in the UK, the Carnival Queen, with women of all skin tones, as part of her antiracist work (Sherwood, 2000). The grassroots Black Power organizer Olive Morris in the 1970s (Sudbury, 1998) and Jayaben Desai's struggle on the picket line at the Grunwick strike (Wilson, 1978) are also part of Black British feminism's narrativization.

Feminist Review 17's special issue on Black British feminism, *Many Voices One Chant: Black Feminist Perspectives* continued to establish the intellectual and activist terrain of Black British feminism. *The Heart of the Race: Black Women's Lives in Britain* (Bryan et al., 1985/2018) charted the grassroots struggles of Black British women in the foundational Black British feminist organization OWAAD (Organization of Women of African and Asian Descent). This organization sought to establish African and Asian descent women's unity as a response to the continued racism in feminism and trade unionism, as well as the sexism in the antiracist movement (Mirza, 2022). *Black*

British Feminism: A Reader (Mirza, 1997) focused on 1990s feminist concerns with decentring identity and incorporating post-modern difference to theorize African and Asian identity as fluid, and fragmented as it interrogated political Blackness (Mirza, 2022). Although these seminal texts established the distinct trajectory of Black British feminism and staked specific claims to what the signifier 'Black' meant in terms of political commitments and movements, continuing activist and intellectual cross-currents maintained links with Black feminism in the USA (Davis and Evans, 2016). Alongside this wellspring of Black feminist theorizing, there were also Black feminist organizations established at local and national levels in a variety of cities, for example, Brixton Black Sisters, OWAAD and Southall Black Sisters in London, Liverpool Black Sisters and the Abasindi Co-operative in Manchester (Watt and Jones, 2015). This rich history of Black feminist organizing in the UK from at least the 1940s is obscured by *Misbehaviour's* focus on the white WLM revealing the film's inherent coloniality which we see played out very overtly on screen through the 1970 Miss World beauty pageant contestants' and white feminists' experiences.

Karen W. Tice's (2021: 317) analysis of beauty pageants as not being just about beauty and bodies is an important point from which to enter the discussion of racialized feminized skin colour politics globally and nationally. For her, beauty pageants

> go beyond flesh and skin to help to define and shape one's sense of self and others. Pageants are deeply rooted in global capitalism, affective, and political economies and they can both reveal and conceal political/personal desires and anxieties central to contestants, sponsors and audiences [...] beauty pageants have tended to affirm and uphold hegemonic discourses and social relations. [...] They construct norms for gendered, classed, and racialized exceptionality and exclusion as well as extoll embodied entrepreneurship, celebrityhood, and cosmopolitanism that can exacerbate and/or attempt to conceal race, cultural, and class divisions [...] but [...] they have also been used as social justice vehicles to promote divergent (and

sometimes counter-hegemonic) agendas to further diasporic, racial, cultural, and sexual identity projects.

Beauty pageants can be both hegemonic and counter-hegemonic, normative and counter-normative, but nevertheless are rooted in capitalism, affect and socio-political life.
The representational politics of beauty are interwoven at the
national and international levels (Banet-Weiser, 1999). For
example, in September 1996, Black Caribbean immigrant
Denny Mendez was crowned Miss Italy, causing consternation
to some because as a Black Caribbean immigrant, she could
not 'represent Italian beauty' (Banet-Weiser, 1999). The case
of Denny Mendez demonstrates that women represent the
nation politically, culturally and morally. Further, 'struggles
over national and international gender identity take place on
beauty pageant stages [...] long conceptualized as good pub-
licity for tourism [... and] a showcase for the formation of
national identity' (Banet-Weiser, 1999: 183–184). Although
categories like femininity carry different meanings when placed
on differentially racialized bodies, other definitions besides
the North-Western also matter in beauty pageants globally.
Zozibini Tunzi, Miss Universe 2019, became the third South
African to win the crown in that remarkable year for Black
women's victories in pageants. She commented that finally
'girls like her' would have different beauty models who 'shared
their faces'. In making this comment, she highlighted the historical anti-Blackness and aesthetic coloniality of Miss Universe and beauty pageants more broadly. We see this theme of
anti-Blackness allied with colonialism in the film *Misbehaviour*.

Misbehaviour (2020, BBC Films/Pathè/Ingenious Pictures/
BFI, Left Bank Pictures Production, Director Philippa Lowthorpe,
Screenplay Gaby Chaippe and Rebecca Frayne; Figure 5.1) is
based on the true story of the inaugural British WLM plot to
disrupt the 1970 Miss World beauty contest. It is also based
in part on Jennifer Hosten's (2020) memoir *Miss World 1970:
How I Entered a Beauty Pageant and Wound Up Making History*.
One of the leaders in this protest was Sally Alexander (Keira
Knightley). My interest here though in thinking through the

Figure 5.1 Pearl Jansen (left) and Jennifer Hosten attending the *Misbehaviour* world premiere, Ham Yard Hotel, Soho, London, PA Image/Alamy.

Black skin affections of love and hate and feminized bodies is not the WLM, but the winner Miss Grenada Jennifer Hosten (Gugu Mbatha-Raw). Jennifer Hosten was the first Miss Grenada at the Miss World beauty pageant and the first Black woman to win. I will also focus on the first runner-up Miss Africa South Pearl Jansen (Loreece Harrison), the first Black South African woman to enter the competition.

Miss Grenada was not the first Caribbean contestant to win Miss World. Jamaica already had a Miss World winner, Carole Joan Crawford in 1963, the year after it became independent from the British Empire (Figure 5.2). She was crowned as Miss Jamaica World and Miss Caribbean World, representing the Anglophone Caribbean region. She could be seen as the first Black Miss World if she is identified as Black Jamaican/

Figure 5.2 Carole Joan Crawford sits on her throne after winning the Miss World 1963 title, Lyceum Ballroom, London, Zuma Press Inc/Alamy.

Caribbean or as the first white Jamaican/Caribbean Miss World if her skin is read as white.

Twenty-three-year-old Hosten had only entered the Miss Grenada contest after she was scouted by the Grenada Tourist Board. Interestingly, this links beauty competitions to island economies in the Caribbean that are economically dependent on tourism, and this dependency continues into the 21st century. Like Joan Crawford, Hosten was also Miss World Caribbean. She entered even though she knew that a Black woman had never won Miss World to that point (Hosten, 2008, 2020). However, neither Hosten nor the other contestants expected the feminist protests which engulfed the competition. After her win, Hosten became an important signifier of beauty for Black women and girls globally (Hosten, 2008, 2020).

The 1970 Miss World contest took place during the Vietnam War and at a time of increasing anti-apartheid politics in the UK and globally. We see a nod to this political landscape when Peter Hain (Luke Thompson) tells Eric Morley (Rhys Ifans) to boycott South Africa's entry, and Morley makes the decision to ask South Africa to send two contestants to the competition – the first ever Black Miss World contestant, Miss Africa South, and Miss South Africa (white). This places anti-Blackness and the skin politics of beauty as a global political issue at the same time as it relegates it to somewhere else (apartheid South Africa), erasing its presence in the UK. Alongside this, the undiscussed backdrop of the Vietnam War, only seen as where Miss World will tour for the troops with US comedian Bob Hope, erases the politics of colonial and neo-imperial occupation globally. Indeed, what this film does in its focus on white women in WLM with those Black women present at meetings and protests as 'extras' rather than leading protagonists, is to attempt to erase accounts not focusing on whiteness, such as Hosten's memoir. On the other hand, Hosten's memoir provides an alter/native (Truillot, 2015) agentic account as a racialized beauty insider/outsider within racial capitalism's (Robinson, 2019, 2021) global white/whitened space of beauty pageants. Global whiteness means that it did not matter that there were women from all over the world in the 50-plus contestants competing. Colonial white British aesthetics, ideas of acceptable, normative femininity and comportment as 'girls' remained. Hosten's and Pearl Jansen's interventions in the film interrupt and lay bare the fact that judgements of global beauty are a function of European colonialism's and neoliberal modernity's 'knowing the other' as familiar strangers.

Both South Africa and Grenada were in the grips of colonialism in 1970. In the 1967 general election, the Grenada United Labour party governed the nation with Eric M. Gairy as the premier. Grenada only became independent from the British Empire on February 7, 1974. Freedom from centuries of white minority rule in South Africa came in 1994 with the end of apartheid and the democratically elected African National Congress government of Nelson Mandela.

Colonialism marked these women's lives from childhood to adulthood.

The film did not deny, of course, that the Miss World contest is a meat market, and we should expect this in a film which centres white British feminist views and women with the privilege and possibility to have 'choices'. The meat market becomes clear when we see Morley at the Miss England competition talking about women's bodies as curves (basically the idealized '36–24–36', which women in the competition struggle to meet as we see when they are measured), boobs, bums and the necessity for contestants to be unmarried, meaning 'untouched'. It is not clear why Miss World has to be a virgin and, if this is a requirement, how it would be enforced or ensured. We must also remember that at this time in the UK's immigration history, 'virginity tests' were deployed at UK borders specifically targeting women from the Indian subcontinent immigrating to the UK as fiancés of British Asian men. Being 'untouched' is also racialized politically as we see here and banning virginity testing, became a focus of Black feminist organizing and theoretical output in the 1970s.

The contestants' curves are checked as each woman is measured in turn for the contest and their 'vital statistics' noted, while their breasts are checked for padding. We also see the focus on curves in the positioning of the cameras in relationship to the stage and the view of the contestants' bodies and faces. As the women walk off the stage, Camera 3 is positioned for what Morley calls the 'derrière' shot so women are seen from all sides by the viewing public, the audience and the judges.

Women compete for the prize money and the hope that they will be able to advance their careers or lives. We see some of this hope for progress when Miss Sweden Maj Christal Johansson (Clara Rosager) is speaking to Miss USA Suki Waterhouse (Sandra Anne Wolsfeld) as the contestants sit in front of a row of mirrors. Miss USA mentions why she entered the contest, the $6,000 prize money and the possibility to earn $30,000 more. For her, this meant that contestants just had to be 'smart' to succeed. Miss Sweden disrupts this deracinated account of the competition with, 'If being smart is all it takes then how come no Black girl has ever won this competition?' She speaks the racism of the pageant from the location of white femininity itself, denying the pageant's neutral meritocracy and beauty as not being about racialized/racializing judgements. Hosten sits next to her to have her hair done, and Miss Sweden says, 'I'm sorry I didn't mean to imply that you couldn't win'. Hosten does not reply. This refusal is itself interesting, as we could say that Miss Sweden, the competition favourite to win, at least has some notion of the anti-Black woman racism in Miss World and was also making a claim for Black women's intelligence as well. Hosten's lack of response does not accept the white race-conscious apology and in so doing refuses both the possibility of 'white fragility' (Di Angelo, 2019) and the potential of a neoliberal move to 'white innocence' (Wekker, 2016). Black refusal, silence, is its own critique of whiteness which refuses to be silenced as the position of privilege from which to speak. We see this struggle for Black women's voices to be heard throughout the film.

This refusal to reply and the other scenes that follow show Hosten's dissidence as she sets about aesthetic reparations, healing the colonial wounds of assumed Black infra-humanity and ugliness. Interestingly, one of the placards of the WLM protestors reads, 'We are not ugly. We're angry'. This highlights the privilege of white skin, as ugliness is already itself racially inflected and does not relate to the white woman's body but sticks tenaciously to Black women's skin. Hosten's dissidence can be seen as global with pro-Black Caribbean roots as she develops decolonial antiracist coalition politics with Miss Sweden and Miss Africa South in the film. In doing this, she both shows love for Blackness and a yearning for Black women and girls' futurity outside of the yoke of colonialism and white supremacy. She also illustrates the impact of mental liberation on one's worldview. This Black woman-centred worldview was wrought through the transnational possibilities of Black feminism in the Anglophone Caribbean that, since the 1930s, had already been the scene of Pan-African feminism by women such as Amy Jacques Garvey and Una Marson. Hosten herself does not reference this, so I call this Black woman centredness because she at no point says she is a Black/Caribbean/Pan-Africanist feminist even whilst she refuses white feminism. We see her turning away from white feminism when she switches off the television when Alexander is doing an interview on beauty pageants as harmful because they make women compete against each other. Her Black woman centrism seeks to decolonize cultural, political and psychic life beginning from a post-enslavement, present anti-colonial perspective by reading and deconstructing racialized gender domination and parsing modes of resistance. What we see Hosten accomplishing in the film is described by Chela Sandoval (2000) as the 'technologies' within 'the methodology of the oppressed'. As they decolonize, these technologies also speak to Black women's and girls' freedom and futurity outside of the confines of the (im)possibilities produced by white supremacy and coloniality.

Sandoval (2000) draws on Fanon's analysis in *Black Skin, White Masks*, which she sees as disrupting the racial hierarchy in the Black/white binary through the technology of the mask and the biology of the skin. Fanon meditates on the skin as Black and the mask of whiteness as a disguise of white power which sets superiority and inferiority askew in the moment one claims one's Black humanness. In that moment, the white mask is removed, replaced by a Black mask. For example, this occurs when Hosten shows her Caribbean colonial, middle-class/elite respectable feminine civility through her profession (flight attendant), her comportment (how she speaks and her serenity – both noted by Miss Sweden) and being properly raised by her parents (middle-class, educated professionals). She refuses any possibility of being thought of as less than any other contestant because of the skin she inhabits and shows that there is Black class differentiation in the colonies.

While the contestants are practising their walk along the stage under Morley's tutelage, Miss Sweden leaves upset, Hosten follows and is let into the room where Miss Sweden is smoking. They share the cigarette, implying some level of intimacy. Hosten asks if she is alright:

MISS SWEDEN: You're so serene. I mean how do you put up with this bullshit?

HOSTEN: You're a very lucky person if you think this is being treated badly. After all you are the favourite to win.

MISS SWEDEN: I don't want to be the favourite if this is what it gets me.

HOSTEN: There is no point swimming against the tide. One just has to rise above it.

MISS SWEDEN: What do you do when you are not being ordered around by a funny English man with strange hair?

HOSTEN: I'm an air hostess but my ambition is to work in broadcasting.

MISS SWEDEN: For real? Or just for them to say, Miss Grenada's ambition is?

HOSTEN: For real.

MISS SWEDEN: You'd be a good broadcaster. You speak so nicely.

HOSTEN: I was properly raised. My father's a lawyer and my mother's a teacher. (Using a different voice perhaps her mother) Elocution and comportment matter, Jennifer.

MISS SWEDEN: I work as a model but I'd like to study. I thought with the prize money I could maybe come to England … but it's all just people pushing you around and flashbulbs in your face the whole time.

HOSTEN: Not so many flashbulbs for me (sounds regretful).

MISS SWEDEN: Like I said it's all bullshit. I mean doesn't it make you angry?

HOSTEN: You know I think maybe it makes me more determined.

We also see here that she begins at the same time to remove the colonial mask through a series of decolonial moves. First, her reading and deconstruction of colonial beauty ideals as racialized as white – 'After all you are the favourite to win'. Second, her critique of white women's racial privilege here and at various points in the film – 'You're a very lucky person if you think this is being treated badly' and continuing in her talk with Miss Sweden, 'Not so many flashbulbs for me (sounds regretful)'. Anger at how one is treated in the misogynoir of the Miss World meat market is even relevant only for white privilege, as she says in answer to Miss Sweden's, 'I mean doesn't it make you angry?', that it makes her more determined. Hosten knows how Black woman's anger would be read negatively as a sign of lack of civility and savagery because of colonial skin colour politics, so this is not an affect which she can display as openly as Miss Sweden. Unlike Miss Sweden, Hosten does not see the competition as 'bullshit' but as opening up career opportunities and political possibilities, as we see at various points in the film.

We see an example of these political possibilities in a scene that we could read as a move by Hosten aimed at removing the colonial mask of whiteness. Hosten presents the possibility of another aesthetic world to Miss Africa South and Black girls, a world where Black women can be Miss World. In this conversation at the party, we see a moment in which Miss Africa South states the reality of the white skin privilege and white aesthetic superiority of her apartheid world. In that world, the biopolitical (Foucault, 1995) and necropolitical (Mbembe, 2019) state controls Black life and death at every level – the social, economic, political, familial and psychic. However, we also see Hosten's decolonial mindset of proclaiming her humanity and determination to rise above the anti-Black woman aesthetic racism in which only white skin matters. She illustrates a decolonial moment of reading white privilege and acting against it by showing her psychic detachment from whiteness and her location of herself as someone who could win just like any other contestant. That is, she disalienates (Césaire, 2000) from whiteness as aesthetics, body, politics, identification and colonial mask.

We do see this attitude of disalienation from the white aesthetic regime when she is in conversation with Miss Africa South at the party attended by the contestants. However, we also see the colonial difference between Hosten's solidly middle-class family life and career and that of a 'coloured South African' who can have a working-class job in a shoe factory under the repressive apartheid regime. We are also made aware that irrespective of the class difference and their geopolitical locations, colonial skin colour politics unites these women. However, apart from the class difference, we also see another colonial difference, a psychic one. This emerges when Miss Africa South questions the possibility of Black women winning Miss World. Hosten as Miss Grenada and Caribbean World never doubts that a Black woman's win is a possibility. She presents it as something that is political because it could make a difference to Miss Africa South's life and the aesthetic location of other Black women and girls within the South African apartheid state. We also see differences in their positioning as colonized women in relation to their nations. Miss Africa South speaks about the repression of the apartheid regime, which would place her in forced exile if she speaks about 'back home' to the media and to anti-apartheid campaigners like Peter Hain. However, Grenada's premier, Sir Eric Gairy, is a member of the panel of judges, and Hosten has no such restraints put on her by the nation that celebrates her win, including by placing her image on a postage stamp:

JANSSEN: This is so nice (commenting about the party where all the contestants are mingling).

HOSTEN: I know. Sometimes I can't believe it's really happening.

JANSSEN: I am a machinist in a shoe factory and then my boss came to say that I was going to London. Everyone on the shop floor was cheering then, standing up and cheered. Now I am here.

HOSTEN: Will it be hard going back?

JANSSEN: I can't talk about that.

HOSTEN: I'm sorry. I didn't mean to pry.

JANSSEN: The authorities warned me. They said if I talk about home they won't let me back. I won't get to see my parents again.

HOSTEN: (in disbelief) What?

JANSSEN Before I got on the plane they showed me photographs of people I'm supposed to have nothing to do with.

HOSTEN: What kind of people?

JANSSEN: Certain journalists, a man called Peter Hain, political people. Home is home (voice breaking) I want to see my parents again (crying) Sorry.

HOSTEN: (smiling empathetically) Maybe home will be different if you're Miss World?

JANSSEN: We're not going to be Miss World (said with certainty, eyes searching Hosten's face).

'We're not going to be Miss World' recognizes the certainty of the shared colonial skin condition of both of them as African descent women. Against all the odds that we see developed in the film as it unfolds with Miss Sweden being the favourite to win, Miss Africa South places second and Hosten wins. One must wonder if the film intimates that this is also a function of the composition of the judges. I say this because, in one scene, we see Julia Morley speaking to Sir Eric Gairy at the Commonwealth Club in London where she is seeing new judges from Asia and Africa. Gairy asks to be included as a judge from the Caribbean as Caribbean, African and Asian judges would make Miss World look 'progressive'. I assume by this he means 'racially progressive', though that is left as an unsaid, so this assumption is based on the regions from which the judges are being drawn, which are parsed as being without white or other racialized populations, as only Black or Indian.

After being crowned Miss World, Jennifer Hosten is in the women's restroom having a much-needed moment of quiet. Sally Alexander has been arrested and is being escorted out of the building by the police. She asks to go to the toilet and sees Hosten there:

ALEXANDER: Sorry, I, oh, oh, you won.

HOSTEN: I thought if I get a moment alone it might just sink in.

ALEXANDER: Wow, congratulations.

HOSTEN: I don't think you mean that.

ALEXANDER: It's not you we're angry at, it really isn't.

HOSTEN: I saw you. You were on the television. You know there'll be little girls watching tonight who'd see themselves differently because I won. Who might just start to believe that you don't have to be white to have a place in the world.

ALEXANDER: I'm glad, I really hope the world opens up for them and for you but making us compete against each other over the way we look, doesn't that make the world narrower for all of us in the end?

HOSTEN: What's your name?

ALEXANDER: Sally.

HOSTEN: Well, Sally, all I say is I look forward to having your choices in life

The police begin banging on the door because Alexander has been too long.

ALEXANDER: Look, I'm really sorry if you are offended in any way.

As the police drag Alexander away, Hosten shouts, 'Please be careful. Don't hurt her'.

Hosten shows the racial Manichean divide in the world as seen from her Caribbean perspective and notes how it has impacted Black aesthetic and social consciousness to the extent that whiteness is still held as superior because Caribbean people still live in coloniality in 1970. What Alexander does not understand is that the world is racially skewed because of the afterlife of enslavement and coloniality, all women are not created equal and race matters to women's lives as lived. Indeed, some women's worlds are narrower than hers because of anti-Black woman racism. Hosten's family background is solidly middle/upper class in Grenada but race makes Alexander more than her in the UK context, a fact which she does not appear to recognize when she includes Hosten in 'all of us'. 'All of us' being that myth of white feminist sisterhood criticized by Hazel Carby (1987), bell hooks (1981) and Audre Lorde (2007a, b), among other Black feminists. Hosten critiques the white neoliberal view of Alexander's choices to illustrate that even choices that might appear to be possible for everyone are racialized and, as a result, choices are inequitably distributed. Hosten refuses Alexander's 'all of us' as she critiques white supremacist feminist epistemologies of ignorance (Mills, 1997) where race does not matter. Race does not matter because only sex and gender politics matter. Further, sex and gender politics

are read from beginning to end from a white woman normative centre. In a typical British neoliberal gesture, Alexander
apologizes for any 'offence caused', refusing to take on board
Hosten's race critique. The film itself ends also refusing to take
Hosten's race critique on board in a celebration of white wom-
en's liberation herstory with the white words on a black screen,
'Attempts to bring down the patriarchy remain ongoing'.

In this decolonial breakthrough critique, Hosten's Black
woman's skin means something other than what the colonial
structures of the British Empire and Miss World pageant would
allow, which would only ever be Fanon's white masks. We see
her deftly manipulating skins. First, with the white colonial
Black woman recognition through practiced Victorian respectable, middle-class comportment. Second, at the same time, she
subverts that through pointing at other means of surviving the
colonial regime of Miss World and the white supremacy of the
colonies and global aesthetics. Third, she creates a space for the
assertion of Black women's humanness through her subversion
itself.

Her victory as Miss World and Miss Africa South as first
runner-up, although within the confines of global white aesthetics, also unsettled the conversation on beauty as only ever
white and Black ugliness as a perpetual condition. It moved
beauty into new psychic, political, social and economic ter-
ritory. This was clearly her intent as she says that she is par-
ticipating for all those Black girls who had never seen this as
a possibility because they could only ever occupy the space of
ugliness of enslavement and its afterlife. Indeed, at the end of
the film, we see her talking animatedly surrounded by young
Black girls in her Grenadan victory reception.

Miss Grenada and Miss Africa South's victories and Hosten's
interventions in the film made clear that decolonization is a
daily activity. She engages in '"de" [as] an active prefix, refer-
ring to a complicated activity of consciousness that undergirds
the operation of the social world, fixes its forms of hierarchy
and power, while undoing its connections to history [which]
aims at transforming all its speaks' (Sandoval, 2000: 85). Here,
Hosten shows that we must read racial domination in objects

as mundane as beauty in order to challenge white supremacy's power and its hold on Black women's and girls' psyches and that of white women's and girls' as well. She enacts a racial democratization of beauty through, 'an ethical ideological code that is committed to social justice according to egalitarian redistributions of power across such differences coded as race, gender, sex, nation, culture or class distinctions' (Sandoval, 2000: 111). Through her decolonial readings and urgings, she disrupts the politics of the Caribbean plantation colony and the apartheid segregation of the shoe factory. Can we see such decolonial continuities in 21st-century Jamaican beauty contestations?

The 21st-century decolonial break in Jamaica?

We have seen in the previous section that Hosten as Miss Grenada and Caribbean World insisted on critiquing whiteness and the anti-Black woman world that it has built based on skin. She does not speak about the plantation pigmentocracy from the Caribbean with which she would be very familiar, nor does Miss Africa South talk about the politics of skin shade in apartheid South Africa. The white supremacy in both of these aesthetic regimes at the time would mean that those who were lighter/white skinned would be seen as more beautiful. I have spoken about this delight in lighter skin elsewhere as a preference for 'mulatticity' (Tate, 2015a) or what T. Denean Sharpley-Whiting (2007) calls 'ethnic ambiguity'. This remains in parts of the world which were in the British Empire and which were built through Indigenous dispossession, chattel slavery and indenture, as was the case in the Caribbean and South Africa (Tate, 2015a). However, what I would like to explore is whether or not we can relegate mulatticity to the past. The discussion that follows focuses on the potential critique of 'the-lighter-the-better-browning' being generated through the darker skin 'browning' embodiment of recent Miss Jamaica beauty queens – Miss Jamaica World and Miss World 2019, Toni-Ann Singh, and Miss Jamaica Universe and Miss Universe 2017 second runner-up, Davina Bennett. It also thinks through whether or not the 2019 sweep of Black winners of beauty pageants means that there has been a democratization of beauty. Or on the other hand, whether or not this is only an instantiation of the commodification and consumption of Black women's bodies in the global skin markets of racial capitalism where Black women's bodies add 'a bit of the other' (hooks, 2014). First, though, let us move to look briefly at the Caribbean's and Jamaica's skin colour politics and race regimes.

In the Caribbean, the colonial state and its race regime have not been dismantled, although there are Black governments in postcolonial/decolonizing post-independence Black countries (Kelly, 2000; Tate and Law, 2015). The political, economic and cultural links of European colonial domination mean that everything that is advanced, civilized and beautiful must be white European or lighter skinned (Tate, 2015a, 2016b, 2020a). This remains in the post-independence Anglophone Caribbean, although there have been alterations (Kelly, 2000), as is unravelled in the discussion in this section. In Jamaica, these alterations have been struggled for by 1930s anti-colonial movements such as Marcus Garvey's United Negro Improvement Association (UNIA), Rastafarianism, Black Power and the continuing evolution of decolonizing 'modern Blackness' (Thomas, 2004) within continuing coloniality in a post-independence state. We can see this continuing coloniality alongside decolonization if we think of the dynamics of this matrix through the prism of skin colour.

In Western Hemispheric post-emancipation, post-indenture societies there is a continuity between enslavement and freedom (Sexton, 2011) in race politics. This continuity is clearly located in the Anglophone Caribbean region's skin colour aesthetics where the centuries-long established axiom has always been 'above all, don't be black' (Gordon, 1997: 63). The 21st-century Caribbean also inhabits and reflects the coloniality of the 'anti-Black world' (Gordon, 2000). The Anglophone Caribbean region does not stand outside it as an exception despite its many multiracial democracies and national narratives, like Jamaica of 'out of many one people' or Trinidad and Tobago's 'all ah we is one' (all of us are one). In this Anglophone Caribbean world, the white, Western bourgeois conception HuMan continues to be *the only possible* human (Wynter, 2003), and Indigenous, Black and People of Colour are still Fanon's (2001) 'wretched of the earth'. Within the wretched of the Black Atlantic world, skin shades and darker African descent skin especially signifies ugliness, poverty, rurality and racial inequality. Skin shade matters because race continues to be a signifier of humanity and privilege in the Anglophone Caribbean. This is the case even if the 'race-mixing' blood quantum categories such as 'sambo', 'mulatto', 'quadroon', 'octoroon' have gone out of popular memory and fallen into linguistic disuse as racially abusive vestiges of colonialism and enslavement. For example, we can see how skin shade matters now and has mattered historically in beauty pageants in Jamaica pre- and post-independence.

Jamaica became independent from the British Empire on August 6, 1962, after more than 300 years of colonial rule. In Jamaica, the 'Ten Types-One People' beauty pageant emerged in 1955 after a colonial history of beauty competitions began in 1929 in which only white women participated (Rowe, 2009, 2013). The Ten Types of 'Jamaican girl' were – Miss Ebony (Black complexion), Miss Mahogany (Cocoa-brown complexion), Miss Satinwood (Coffee and milk complexion), Miss Golden Apple (Peaches and cream complexion), Miss Apple Blossom (European parentage), Miss Pomegranate (White-Mediterranean parentage), Miss Sandalwood (Pure Indian parentage), Miss Lotus (Pure Chinese parentage), Miss Jasmine (Part-Chinese parentage) and Miss Allspice (Part-Indian parentage) (Rowe, 2013: 122). Beauty contests from 1929 to 1954 were then about inscribing white racial dominance within colonial Jamaica, including at the level of aesthetics. In 1955, the 'Ten Types' competition was held to recognize the multiplicity in the racial backgrounds of Jamaicans. There were ten separate competitions, with each discursively constructed category related to a specific 'racial skin'. The winners were produced who would reign as queens because they were all the most beautiful exemplars of that racial group of Jamaicans. For example, 'Miss Ebony', 'Miss Appleblossom' and 'Miss Allspice', among other racial categories, were intended to showcase Jamaican multiracial identity to make a claim that it was a colonial nation that had overcome race through the assimilation of all its peoples into a fledging pre-independence democracy (Rowe, 2009, 2013). Interestingly, all of the categories are food items such as Allspice or, like Jasmine, relevant for consumption whether as wood or flower. Some of the categories are also located globally outside of Jamaica while being within it – Lotus, Sandalwood, Pomegranate, Apple Blossom, Ebony. Up to this point in Jamaican beauty history, all darker-skinned women, irrespective of ancestry, had been invisible as icons of feminine desirability. The 'Ten Types' pageant's Miss Ebony presented, 'the possibility of a desirable and respectable black femininity that an entire community of dark-skinned, black-identified Jamaicans, both male and female, could invest in and were expected to aspire towards' (Rowe, 2013: 124). 'Ten Types' also universalized Western feminine standards by showing that irrespective of race, Jamaican women could conform to a recognizable colonial ideal of bodily slenderness, as well as respectable middle-class comportment revealed in English language use and educational/professional levels.

Black nationalists used 'gendered constructs to renegotiate race, specifically African-descended racial identities, to infer Jamaica's departure from colonialism and entrance into the modernity of new nations' (Rowe, 2013: 118). By 1959, the Miss Jamaica pageant had begun to crown light-skinned brown winners, an aesthetic position which was subject to public critique because of colour discrimination (Rowe, 2013). This critique led to the setting up in the 1960s of a rival to the Miss Jamaica pageant, Miss Jamaica Nation, and the crowning of middle-class, professional, darker-skinned Yvonne Whyte as its first winner. She had a large fan base among Black Jamaicans and visited the independence celebrations in Malawi as Jamaica's cultural ambassador (Rowe, 2013). Cultural nationalism was articulated through the pageants, and nationalists helped to 'create iconic imagery of black femininity', mobilizing it as a political tool for Black liberation struggles (Rowe, 2013: 129). Jamaican beauty pageants have always been sites of racial, colour and class contestation in a society in which colourism means light skin brownness is preferred, even whilst 'the typical Jamaican Out of Many One People' women, Miss Jamaica World/Miss Jamaica Universe are presented as *national* representatives and cultural ambassadors (Rowe, 2013).

In Western Hemispheric cultural consciousness and representations, the darker-skinned Black African descent woman continues to be a marginalized skin aesthetic deriving from shared North Atlantic universals (Truillot, 2015), as said earlier in the book. The colonial aesthetic gaze continually reproduces darker African descent skin as (un)desirable but hypersexualized (Fanon, 1986; Wilder, 2010; Yancy, 2008). 'Racial capital' (Hunter, 2021) continues to attach to lighter skin especially on women's bodies because the Western Hemisphere still operates within the anti-Black African descent darker-skinned woman, negative aesthetic regime. The weight of this historical and contemporary anti-Blackness leads us to the question of whether or not aesthetic decolonization is actually possible because of the pervasiveness of colourism.

From the perspective and location of the US, Margaret Hunter (2021: 86–87) states that colourism is:

> a structural system of discrimination that uses the status of skin tone to differentiate and value racialized bodies. Light-skinned people of color experience privilege in this system and dark-skinned people experience discrimination. The forms and intensity of that discrimination are affected by other aspects of their identity such as gender identity and presentation, sexuality, language use, economic class status, education level, and more. Colorism is not a stand-alone system. It is built on the foundation of structural racism [it] is a manifestation of racism [...] people of all races practice colorism. [...] Colorism is a much larger system that permeates not just the United States, but global media culture. Because colorism is a subsystem of structural racism, it operates in many institutions and does not require the actual presence of racist individuals [...] in this way, people of color feel the effects of white racism in their communities even when no white people are present.

Based on structural racism, colourism is institutionalized and systemic. This means that people of all 'races' practice colourism, and it is a transracial phenomenon that attaches value to different skin colours within a global pigmentocracy. I am specifically interested in the case of Jamaican views on beauty and skin shade – and I began some of that exploration earlier – because Jamaican pageant winners will be the focus of skin affections here.

In Jamaica, there have been debates on beauty since at least the 1930s, with many vocally refusing the preference for whiteness even before independence in 1962 (Barnes, 1994). We saw that in the brief look at Jamaica's pageant history earlier. The public debate on colourism was initiated and invigorated by an anti-colonial impetus and decolonial worldview from the 1930s in Rastafarianism, Marcus Garvey and the UNIA. Clearly, this periodization could also extend further back into Jamaican history with the first slave revolts as well as maroonage because uprising and fleeing plantation life to set up free Black communities already instantiate anti-colonial politics and decolonization in terms of enslavement and Black freedom. The 1930s decolonization of prevailing colonial aesthetics through Rastafarianism, Garveyism and Black Nationalism was focused on the valorization of Blackness, African descent darker skin, natural hair and more 'African features'. This aesthetic decolonization continued into Black Power in the 1970s. In Marcus Garvey's (1923) *An Exposé of the Caste System among Negroes*, he criticizes what he calls the privilege of 'the caste of colour' in US America, the Caribbean and Africa. He also sets out the UNIA programme in terms of skin colour, which was in marked contrast to the prevailing plantation pigmentocracy in Jamaica at that time.

Garvey's Pan-Africanist pragmatic political focus is on building 'the race' irrespective of skin shade. I say pragmatic here because he is alive to the differences in skin that exist in the Black diaspora as a result of its histories of transracial heterosexual reproductive 'race mixing'. For him, being 'mixed race' does not make one less Black. Blackness is a political project based on attachment forged through the adversities and vagaries of plantation pigmentocracy's 'one-drop rule'. He uses white supremacy's negation of Blackness as a means of affirming Black political and identity ends. We see this as Garvey points out that the task for 'the race' is to build itself irrespective of skin colour differences because all Black people are 'racially just alike':

> The program of the Universal Negro Improvement Association is that of drawing together, into one universal whole, all the Negro peoples of the world, with prejudice toward none. We desire to have every shade of color, even those with one drop of African blood, in our fold; because we believe that none of us as we are, is responsible for our birth; in a word we have no prejudice against ourselves in race. [...] We believe that every Negro racially is just alike, and therefore, we have no distinction to make, hence wherever you see the UNIA you will find us giving every member of the race an equal chance and opportunity to make good [...] Unfortunately, there is a disposition on the part of a certain element of our people in America, the West Indies and Africa, to hold themselves up as the 'better class' or 'privileged' group on the caste of color [...] Whether we are light, yellow, black or what not, there is but one thing for us to do, and that is to get together to build up a race.
>
> (Garvey, 1968: 68–73)

Garvey's philosophy on 'building a race' sat uneasily alongside colonial Jamaica's continuation of the white/light brown aesthetic preference and its intricate relationship to class politics. Here, light or white skin and non-African descent marked on skin, hair and facial features was for the most part a signifier of middle-/elite-class status.

Skin colour and hair texture were also a focus in the decolonial Black aesthetics of Jamaican Pan-African feminist Una Marson (1905–1965). Jamaican playwright, poet, activist and Britain's first Black feminist writer Una Marson's (1937) poem, 'Kinky hair blues' where she avers 'I like me Black face and me

kinky hair', highlights how early 20th-century British imperial aesthetics shaped Black women's bodily surfaces as well
as the psychic violence of its imperatives. In line with Fanon
(2021), this shaping has to be resisted through assertions of *love
of the self*. 'To like' in Jamaica is 'to love'. To say that as a Black
woman colonial subject one loves one's Black face and kinky
hair is already a decolonial movement away from the violence
of colonial aesthetics towards self-love. This poem calls to
Black women in the British Caribbean colonies and beyond
to remove the white colonial mask. It asks that they disalienate
from the skins produced by colonialism, to shed that blackness of always already known inferiority, and emerge anew as
Black, free from colonial skins and their demand that hair be
straightened and skin be bleached. Written in Jamaican Creole
(Patois), it spoke linguistic and ontological liberation from the
givens of blackness in British colonialism. The linguistic given
was that only British English should be strived for, written and
published because Patois and other Anglophone Caribbean
Creole languages could only ever be 'broken English' not languages in their own right. The reading from language to people could be extended to the ontological colonial given that
like the language Black Jamaicans were also broken and perpetually enslaved/colonized subjects. It also spoke to the Jamaican
aesthetic condition. Specifically, that of straight/straightened
hair and lighter skin as aesthetic ideal especially in terms of
heterosexual intimacies. The force of this ideal is so great that
even if one does not envy women with straighter hair, and
instead loves their God-given Black face and kinky hair, one
has to deny one's bodily affective attachments in order not to
be 'left on the shelf' and to fit into acceptable, desirable, heterosexual femininity. She ends her poem with self-affirmation as
she speaks against societal negation of kinky hair and dark skin:

> Lord 'tis you did gie me (Lord it's you who gave me)
> All dis kinky hair. (All this kinky hair)
> 'Tis you did gie me
> All dis kinky hair,
> And I don't envy gals (girls)

What got dose loose locks so fair. (Who have loose hair
so fair)
I like me black face (I like my Black face)
And me kinky hair. (And my kinky hair)
I like me black face
And me kinky hair,
But nobody loves dem (them),
I jes don't tink it's fair. (I just don't think it's fair)

(Marsen, 1937)

As said previously, colonial aesthetics such as these were also
linked to class. This colour-class relation was taken forward to
independence in 1962 and beyond. At that point in Jamaica's
history, the creole multiracial project subsumed in the national
motto 'Out of Many One People', consolidated around a
turn to Africa and a cultural policy focused on African heritage (Thomas, 2004). The political break from Europe on
independence, invocations of the importance of Africa and
African-Jamaican historical struggles and the validation of
Black popular cultural practices did not bring an end to aesthetic colonialization as we see in Carole Joan Crawford being
crowned Miss Jamaica and Caribbean World in 1963. Jamaican
whiteness was replaced by Jamaica's 'browning' by the 1980s.
'Browning' marked the beginning of modern Blackness in
20th-century Jamaica. Therefore, rather than being linked to
colonial aesthetic race/class hierarchies browning was a modern Blackness aesthetic, a divergence from the centuries-long
ideal of the white/very light brown phenotype (Mohammed,
2000; Tate, 2016b). In previous writing (Tate, 2016, 2016b), I
have claimed that the 'ing' in browning accomplishes a specific
task through race performativity. That is, 'ing' in this aesthetic
ideal shows that browning is an achieved aesthetic. We are not
born into browning because of 'brown' skin, so anyone can
potentially be a browning through aesthetic practices.

However, it must be said that Jamaica's pigmentocracy bind-
ing class to skin colour and relegating darker skin to the bottom
of the aesthetic hierarchy continues (Brown-Glaude, 2007; Tate,
2016, 2016b; Hope, 2009). We see this aesthetic hierarchy being

critiqued in Jamaican dancehall singer Spice's 2018 hit 'Black Hypocrisy' and also a backlash against what many in Jamaica saw as her appearing to have 'bleach out' (bleached) her skin in her promotional material. This backlash relates to Jamaican modern Blackness aesthetics and after negative comments on Jamaican social media, she admitted her skin had not been bleached (https://www.capitalxtra.com/news/videos/spice-skin-bleaching-love-hip-hop-trailer Accessed 1/25/2022).

Figure 5.3 Portrait of Spice in Kingston, Jamaica.

The video for 'Black Hypocrisy' and the lyrics are teachable moments in terms of continuing anti–darker-skinned Black aesthetics hidden by browning as a Black originated, putatively democratizing beauty model. In the video, Spice speaks to a skin consciousness-raising class with other Black darker-skinned women with motivational and darker-skinned Black beauty experience placards that read:

> Black hypocrisy, respect due to my strong melanin/ Demolish colourism – Stop racism/I am dripping melanin with honey/I am Black without apology/Black girls lose self-confidence because of you/Dem say mi black till mi shine till mi look dirty/B beautiful/L lovely/A attractive/C courageous/K kind/A Black woman once told me that I am too Black.

The class go on a march through the streets with the placards. Leading the march, Spice critiques racism and colourism (Bun (burn) racism, demolish colourism). She sees colourism as hate by Black people (I get hate from my own race). This causes low self-esteem in girls when 'piiple dem seh (the people say) I'm too Black', and 'dem seh mi black til mi shine, til mi luk dirty (they say I am so Black that I am shiny and I look dirty). Black colourism's hate occurs if it is only the browning ideal that can be beautiful. It is this hypocrisy within Spice's song which produces 'dirty inequity'. As she sings:

> Mi luv di way mi look (*I love the way I look*)/Mi luv (*I love*) mi pretty Black skin/Respect due to mi (*my*)strong melanin/Proud a mi colour, luv di skin that I'm in/Bun racism, demolish colourism/

> Black piiple hypocrisy/It leave di girls dem with low self-esteem/Unu gwaan like seh yuh haffi brown fi pretty (*You act as if you have to be brown to be pretty*)/Fuck di (*the*) whole of dem (*them*) dirty inequity.

Spice unequivocally denounces anti-Black darker-skinned aesthetic racism in Jamaica (Tate and Law, 2015) and demonstrates how very deeply engrained it is within the national psyche. We also see this in the experiences of Jamaica's national son, multiple Olympic champion Usain Bolt OJ[1], former spokes-body for Puma, Nissan and Virgin Media and global sporting icon. He has faced classism and racism from elite Jamaicans notwithstanding his global celebrity and current US dollar multi-millionaire status, after being listed in the *Forbes* Rich List. He has experienced what he calls their strong 'bad mind',[2] for example, from his neighbours in the housing complex where he lived in Upper St Andrew, but support from other Jamaicans. Bolt said, 'A lot of them, because dem go school and work years and years fi reach and me jus come up and because of sports mi get everything, dem nuh happy. [...] The ghetto yutes dem and everybody else love me and happy fi si me'[3] (Johnson, 2016).

Colourism has been obvious in the 'face of the nation' in Jamaica in Miss Jamaica World and Miss Jamaica Universe beauty contests throughout the 20th century, although the 'Ten Types' Jamaican view of its people still dominated (Rowe, 2009). Jamaican women have usually been chosen in the contests with an eye within the competitions to what skin, look, hair, sells globally. Remember beauty pageants are also big business, embedded in global racial capitalism and essential for tourism's selling of countries as desirable destinations through the bodies of their women nationals. However, two 21st-century beauty queen choices make us wonder if 'browning' can now be shades darker than the 20th-century fixation on 'lighter skin'. I will look at the skins of Miss Jamaica and Miss World 2019, Toni-Ann Singh and Miss Jamaica Universe and Miss Universe second runner-up 2017, Davina Bennett, in order to think about this and to speculate about colourism's continuation versus a 21st-century shade openness in Jamaican beauty pageants. That is, I want to initiate a discussion on whether these darker-skinned beauty queens demonstrate an aesthetic decolonization from below forged through modern Blackness producing a societally accepted extension of the skin shades of the browning archetype.

'Miss Jamaica World' and 'Miss Jamaica Universe' beauty contestants evolved from colonial white-only beauty contests among Jamaica's elite in the 1930s, through to the 'Ten Types, One People' beauty contest acknowledging Jamaica's racial diversity (Rowe, 2009). 'The face of the nation' played out in Miss Jamaica World (winner of the pageant) and Miss Jamaica

Universe (second runner-up) is an annual site of audience contestation with national racial identity politics also being centred as the nation imagines itself and its racial future through the pageants. Traditionally white/'light skin' brown, straight/straighter haired beauty has been preferred to represent the country (Barnes, 1994), for example, Carole Joan Crawford (Miss Jamaica and Miss Caribbean and Miss World 1963), Cindy Lou Breakspeare (Miss Jamaica and Miss World 1976) and Lisa Hanna (Miss Jamaica and Miss World 1993). We see an interruption to this with Toni-Ann Singh's crowning as both Miss Jamaica and Miss World 2019.

Figure 5.4 Miss World 2019 Toni-Ann Singh of Jamaica celebrates winning the Miss World final in London, Britain, December 14, Reuters/Alamy.

For the first time in the history of the Miss Jamaica competition, darker-skinned browning winners emerged in the 21st century. Dreadlocked Zahra Redwood was Miss Jamaica Universe in 2007, and Afro-haired Davina Bennett was Miss Jamaica Universe in 2017. Their skins undermined the dominance of the aesthetic ideal of white/lighter skin and straight/straighter hair. This continued with Khadijah Robinson, Miss Jamaica World, 2018, with lighter skin Emily Madison placing second as Miss Jamaica Universe. Miss Jamaica World 2019 Toni-Ann Singh became Miss World in December 2019 but lighter skin Iana Tickle Garcia was second as Miss Jamaica Universe. Singh, with a Jamaican Indian father and a Jamaican African descent mother, was the fourth Jamaican to win Miss World in 2019. She reigned for two years because the Covid-19 pandemic meant that no Miss World contest was held in 2020. Do these women as the face of the Jamaican nation signal a rupture in the hegemony of colonial aesthetics?

The break as a rupture in colonial aesthetics?

Zahra Redwood and Davina Bennett won praise for their natural hair – locks and Afro, respectively – and darker skin. Although Redwood did not place, Bennett was second runner-up in the Miss Universe 2017 competition. Her Afro hairstyle 'broke the internet', and her fans started the hashtag #MissJamaicaShouldHaveWon. National and global aesthetic inclusion such as this recasts darker African descent skin as a valuable and loved diasporic asset rather than hated colonial object. In Jamaica, clearly, there are darker-skinned browning beauty models who have been re-valued, producing another racialized beauty hierarchy from below through modern Blackness. This re-valuation begins from the darker shades of browning, a specifically Jamaican 21st-century construction undermining coloniality's white/lighter skin aesthetic regimes. We can say though that even within this potential decolonial change, shadism as browning approximation is still relevant as it relates to international beauty pageants, part of racial capitalism's objectification and consumption of Black women's bodies. If this is so, then this continues colonial aesthetic hierarchies and a colonial politics of skin values and devaluations irrespective of the inclusion of darker browning skin.

As Spice reminds us, ideas of darker African descent skin as ugly circulate through colourism. These ideas remain within modern Blackness as shadism's 'second skin' (Cheng, 2011). This second skin still textures the politics of hypervisibility of the darker-skinned African descent woman in Jamaica, mapping onto 'brown'/lighter skin colour preferences in the Caribbean and Black Atlantic diaspora. We can say though that Redwood, Bennet and Singh show that there has been *limited* 'reversal of that epistemology of ignorance which places lighter skin first in the racialized skin hierarchy' (Tate, 2016: 120) within the local-global skin markets of Miss Jamaica World and Miss Jamaica Universe. However, we cannot begin to celebrate a 'post-race' or utopic deracialized aesthetic future/present if we bear in mind Hunter's assertion that colourism does not need the presence of racist individuals with People of Colour feeling the effects of anti-Blackness and misogynoir in the absence of white people. This is the present racialized gender aesthetic life of coloniality as lived by Black women and girls.

What is now needed for Jamaican aesthetic futures is to continue to turn away from the last vestiges of colonial Black skin hate through Césaire's (2000) disalienation, as we see in the rise of darker skin browning in Jamaican aesthetic hierarchies. This is a movement towards Black beauty experience and a Black worlding of the aesthetic world where the HuMan would have to be remade to include all shades of African descent. Garvey already told us this was necessary in the 1930s, as we saw earlier in this chapter. The aesthetic decolonization of the mind is important when everything good, civilized, beautiful is measured in European terms in the Western Hemisphere (Kelly, 2000). Césaire (2000) asks that we dream ourselves out of domination as we plot a course out of coloniality. Jamaican modern Blackness has begun to do that, removing skin from plantation aesthetics as it charts the outlines of Black women's skin futurities.

Conclusion

This chapter used the politics of skin in beauty pageants as its central focus in order to engage in a discussion of skin and beauty within the Western Hemisphere and the Anglophone Caribbean. Reading the film *Misbehaviour*, the discussion showed the possibilities of Black women's resistance to global, colonial beauty hierarchies. Focusing on Jamaica as a decolonizing state, it then took as its central question the possibility of a 'break' in colonial lighter/white skin beauty iconicity. It did this to interrogate whether this means an end to colonial hate of Black skin in the 21st century or points to its continuation in the global consumption of lighter Black skin as a marker of 'post-race' anti-Black racism in the Global North-West and South-West. It highlighted the fact that what counts as beautiful locally is also inflected by global markets in Black women's skins. Beauty pageants nationally and internationally are big business, and for countries dependent on tourism, as is the case for most of the Anglophone Caribbean, their nation's face has to have global appeal. It has to sell as commodity. The examples of *Misbehaviour*, darker-skinned browning beauty pageant winners in Jamaica and globally and Spice's critique of anti-darker-skinned colourism point to how Black women continue to disrupt an aesthetic system which is stacked against them. They do this by disalienating from the colonial givens of beauty/ugliness as read through skin and ascribing that skin with positive affect rather than the negation of the anti-Black psyche. The discussion also shows how Black counter-publics in nations like Jamaica do this work of affirming Black beauty futurities by refusing whiteness even whilst colourism is a part of its affective texture and identification lifeblood. Indeed, colourism means we cannot say that there has been an end to colonial hate of darker skin even in the 21st century. Skin liberation is not yet at hand although it is long-awaited.

Notes

1 The Order of Jamaica is a state honor established in 1969 and is conferred on Jamaican citizens of outstanding distinction.
2 Wishing that only negative things happen to someone; envy.
3 A lot of them because they go to school and work years and years to become successful and I am newly successful because sports has given me everything, they are not happy. [...] The ghetto youths and everybody else love me and are happy to see me.

6 Conclusion

Intersectional skin still matters:
thinking in Black

Introduction

> *For the master's tools will never dismantle the master's house.*
> They may allow us temporarily to beat him at his own
> game, but they will never enable us to bring about gen-
> uine change. And this fact is only threatening to those
> women who still define the master's house as their only
> source of support [...] divide and conquer must become
> define and empower.
>
> (Lorde, 2007b: 106)

Audre Lorde's words speak to the very heart of why Black feminist decolonial cultural criticism is necessary. I read Lorde's words
as a Black lesbian feminist critique of white hetero-patriarchy
and white feminism as structural and systemic dominations.
Lorde seeks to critique the colonial racialized power dynamics
of divide and conquer along the lines of race and gender and
to produce something different through Black feminist meditations on colonial power/knowledge. That is, to *define* knowledge within the disciplinary canons as already racialized and
colonized, *define* the systemic and institutionalized workings
and impacts of racism, sexism and homo-/trans-phobia and
to *empower* those racialized, gendered others who are or have
been traditionally marginalized. For example, those who have
been refused the position of knower and knowledge producer
which means that in terms of empowerment we should centre

DOI: 10.4324/b23223-6

excluded epistemologies and ontologies rather than recycling the Eurocentric canon which functions to keep in place the colonial ideology that Blackness equates to unreason.

In 'On the Monstrous Threat of Reasoned Black Desire', Lewis Ricardo Gordon (2014) takes up this ideology of Blackness = unreason. Gordon looks at the existing incompatibility between the concepts 'reason' and 'Black' which Frantz Fanon had already elucidated in *Black Skin, White Masks* because of the colonization of reason by whiteness as a structure of domination. In the Western Hemisphere, we must speak our 'concerns of freedom in a world where colonialism and racism dominate even the production of knowledge' (Gordon, 2014: 180). As Fanon, Wynter, Césaire, Hall and Gordon (2014: 183), among others show, there is a white, colonial 'narcissistic investment in a false image. While there is hatred of black people, there is a pervasive love of Negroes […] while Black and African philosophers assert black and African Diasporic *thought*, the demands of a white dominated, antiblack academy is to have Negro *entertainment* […] so-called mainstream theory and scholarship demand leaving the thinking (and by extension, theorizing) to whites'.

This book has engaged in fugitivity/maroonage/errantry *in reading* Black skin's intersectional cultural life as liberation thinking, taking up Gordon's (2014: 184) assertion that 'thinking and seeing require doing so in black'. This approach to reading engages US Afropessimism (fugitivity) and Anglophone and Hispanophone (maroonage) and Francophone (errantry) Caribbean decolonial thinking as a mooring for thinking and seeing 'in Black'. Seeing and thinking 'in Black' through fugitivity, maroonage and errantry show a desire to escape and transgress the confines of the plantation read as the normative boundaries of the canons of academic knowledge within what Barnor Hesse (2014: 288) calls 'the hegemonic effects of colonial-racial foreclosure which refuses to think the colonial-racial formations of thought'. Instead, there is a, 'preemptive exclusion of possible references and their locutions from the realm of the symbolic, the field of representation or discourse […] which forecloses the possibility of particular representations' (Hesse, 2014: 290). Indeed, this equates to treating the foreclosed as 'if it did not exist' (Hesse, 2014: 290).

This restriction of what it is possible to think or say occurs on a daily basis but often goes unnoticed and unremarked because of hegemonic anti-Black knowledge systems. For example, Black and reason being seen as binaries is a colonial-racial foreclosure which enables Black thought to not be perceived as theory that can be universal in academic life. Again, for example, sanitizing 'race' by replacing it with 'ethnicity' or saying it is a social construct (which it is, of course) erases the fact that we should understand race 'politically as a constituted, relational, Western colonial category of governance' which cannot be 'dissociated from its modern colonial formation in relations of violence, regulation and administration' (Hesse, 2014: 295). Thinking and seeing in Black, that is, refusing colonial-racial foreclosure, already produces the *'reading into* fugitivity/maroonage/errantry' mentioned at the beginning of the book as integral to Black feminist decolonial thought. Such thought transgresses the colonial-racial foreclosure within coloniality that theorizing and envisaging the world is the terrain of whiteness alone. Black feminist decolonial thought, 'just won't act right no matter how much the power of [normative white] judgement tries to make it "well behaved" [… to] attempt to ensure equilibrium' (Moten, 2018: 1). Instead, it is insistently off-kilter to facilitate thinking and seeing in Black.

Thinking and seeing in Black

For the master's tools will never dismantle the master's house. Lorde's injunction is Black feminist decolonial resistance which most emphatically should not be read as white feminism's 'parasitic underside' (Moten, 2018: 4). This resistance avers the incommensurability of what Wilderson 111 (2010) calls 'the grammars of suffering' of the enslaved and the masters, the colonizers and the colonized. Lorde's is a 'radical sociality of the imagination […] the free irruption of thought […] inseparable from the racialization and sexualization [and gendering and intersectionality] of the imagination' (Moten, 2018: 4) Thus, it is that a challenge:

such as thinking [and seeing] in black requires taking on the constructions of knowledge in the modern world as both a liberatory enterprise and an epistemic critique of a peculiar kind, for in effect, the radical claim would be about failures at the heart of the production – and conceptions – of knowledge that have become hegemonic (now 'traditional') and about the resources available (the underside, the black side of modern thought) to transcend them.

(Gordon, 2014: 184)

Black feminist decolonial thought is a practice of liberation which seeks to go beyond the taken-for-granted ideas of colonial knowledge systems and praxis. It is reading, thinking and seeing from a Black intersectional perspective which refuses the black homology produced by racist second skin discourses and which insists on the need to theorize Black skin's affective life in the Western Hemispheric world. Black feminist decolonial thinking in Black has been developed here through intersectional analyses of skin colour politics in cultural representation that aim to resist colonial-racial foreclosure. The challenge has been throughout not to produce colonial reifications of blackness by asserting a paraontological distinction between coloniality's black and Black people/women, children, men/community. Here coloniality's black calls anti-Blackness into being as it recycles the enslavement past's 'flesh'. However, thinking and seeing in Black resists the racialized gender othering of 'flesh'. To go back again to Moten (2018: 242), what is resisted is Blackness coming 'into relief against the backdrop of its negation, which takes the form of epidermalizatin, of a reduction of some to flesh, and to the status of no-bodies, so that some others can stake their impossible claim upon bodies and souls'.

The book has spent many words and several chapters thinking and seeing in Black in discussing raced and gendered skin and its affective life. Even more specifically, it discussed Black skin's intersectional life within popular culture representations, including what Blackness means and some of what Black people and communities experience because of the meanings of skin. It looked at how Sylvia Wynter's HuMan (as white) continues to ensure that in enslavement's afterlife, blackness resumes its colonial life of infrahumanity as exchangeable commodity and fungible property (Gilroy, 2004; Hartman, 1997; Wilderson, 2010; Wilderson and King (2020); Sexton, 2011; Sharpe, 2010).

Drawing on Fanon (2021), the analyses looked at Black skin as gendered historico-racial and epidermal racial schema with a discursive, organic, social, political, affective and psychic life, historically and contemporaneously. Looking at Black skin as gendered historico-racial and epidermal racial schema demanded a contextualization within the Black Atlantic diaspora and the Western Hemisphere as the scene of the emergence of the designation black for people of African descent. We also saw that 'Africa as black' stands in relation to 'Europe as white' and its creation of difference, of those others set apart from itself and that this began most likely from Ancient Greece and Rome. We can argue about origins, of course, but what is certain is that blackness as it is presently constituted, experienced and lived within Western Hemispheric cultural life as negation and unfreedom emerged from centuries of enslavement, colonialism and its aftermath. We can see this continuation if we think about Orlando Patterson's idea that slavery is a relational dynamic rather than historical instances within specific places and spaces (Park, 2020).

Indeed, Frank B. Wilderson 111 reminds us that, 'Africans went into the ships and came out Blacks [...because of white] conversion of the incomprehensible African into the comprehensible Negro' (Wilderson 111 and King, 2020: 38–41). As said earlier in the book, this genealogy has produced discursive second skins which engulf Black individuals with their always already known of what blackness should be and/or can become. These discursive second skins that are present within analyses of cultural representations have been argued to be intersectional in terms of race and gender in conversation with Frantz Fanon, Stuart Hall and Sylvia Wynter, amongst others. We have seen some of these intersectional race and gender second skins that have been looked at through the vehicle of analyses of representations in the examples throughout the book on modelling, films, beauty pageants, men's grooming advertisements and Black/white blackface, for example. The discussion has also looked at 21st-century re-inscriptions of Blackness, for example, in beauty pageants as national and individual subjectivities are re-narrated through changes in Black beauty's iconic skins.

In the thinking and seeing in Black that emerged in the aforementioned analyses, intersectionality has *not* been viewed as a 'post-Black feminist' idea – a term related only to Kimberlé Crenshaw's seminal work – nor an 'ideograph' that stands in for scholarship that looks at the oppression of Black women and women of colour (Bilge, 2020). Intersectionality has been located firmly within US Black feminist thought, which has been impacted by other racialized feminisms and liberation movements (Alexander-Floyd, 2012; Bilge, 2020; Nash, 2018). Intersectional readings from a Black feminist decolonial viewpoint also necessitated the inclusion of the tools of Black Latin American and Hispanophone Caribbean (BLAHC) decolonial feminists, such as Ochy Curiel and Yuderkys Espinosa Miñoso, and Anglophone Caribbean feminist and decolonial thinkers, such as Una Marson.

Thus, in engaging with the intersectionality of Black skin as raced and gendered object and colonial/colonized artefact, the book has resisted the erasure of the labour of Black feminists in the Western Hemisphere in its development of the outlines of what a Black feminist decolonial reading of intersectional Black skin representations entails. Therefore, the book has resisted what Sirma Bilge (2020) describes as intersectionality's vulnerability to being stripped of its Black feminist origins and become a 'fungible object' through which other academic agendas are developed and sustained. It has also resisted the impulse to understand intersectionality as relevant only for US Black feminist theory, as its 'home space', and instead, it sees intersectionality as a central concern for the Western Hemispheric Black feminist decolonial emotional and political labours of theorizing and activism historically and now. The discussion has also spent time developing various theoretical pathways to constructing a Black feminist decolonial approach to cultural criticism and analysis, thinking through Black skin's affective life. It has also worked towards constructing intersectionality as an approach to thinking that is *intrinsically* decolonial because of its Black diaspora feminist activist, political and theoretical interventions. Intersectionality is intrinsically decolonial because it turns away from Eurocentric knowledge and world/subjectivity making. In turning away from Eurocentrism, intersectionality engages in a Césairean disalienation which produces new knowledges, subjectivities, politics and affects as it unseats the traditional canon. The book has thought both *through*, *with* and *along the grain of* a Black feminist decolonial lens in its analyses of Black skin as intersectional in terms of race and gender.

The analyses have shown that a Black feminist decolonial approach to cultural representation seeks to go beyond the white colonial psyche which we have all inherited and live within in the Western Hemisphere. As such, it takes up Glissant's (1997) challenge that we must refuse to be thought or to think ourselves through the colonizer/colonized opposition of empire because it is only then that decolonization will begin. It is clear that decolonization is also thinking and seeing in Black and demands acknowledgement of imbrication and implication in anti-Blackness on the way to Black feminist decolonial thinking.

If we think about Charles Mills' (1997) racial contract and its epistemologies of ignorance and Michel Foucault's (1980b) power/knowledge, we can see how we are imbricated and implicated in anti-Blackness within the Western Hemisphere and beyond, irrespective of the skin we inhabit. A Black feminist decolonial approach of thinking and seeing in Black *unsettles* as it moves across skin colour politics and *decentres* the givens of social, political, economic, affective and psychic life. Its movement creates crises within the skin politics of whiteness and the colourism of Black communities in terms of what happens when we unearth and refuse the recognition politics of racist stereotypes of Black lighter/darker skin. One key element of this refusal is asserting common harm from anti-Black racism and misogynoir irrespective of skin tone. This is the turning away from, or Césaire's disalienation from, anti-Blackness, which has been argued is key to Black feminist decolonial thought and praxis. The book began in a particular space and time of Black pain, and I want to return to that now by meditating briefly on what it means to live with the pain of trauma because of anti-Blackness. This accomplishes the necessary political step of taking Black skin politics beyond the libidinal economy of racialized gender representation which has been the main focus of the book, although that has been very generative in helping us think intersectionally through the racialized gender affects of skin and flesh.

Black skin politics beyond representation

Skin matters. It impacts our intersectional lives as lived. *Black skin as flesh* shouldn't be seen as organic matter but as the building block of national racial structuration across the Western Hemisphere. One socio-political, historical and contemporary artefact that enables us to see the racialized gender dynamics of skin is cultural representations. Analyses of racialized gender representations enabled us to see the everyday life of the politics of anti-Black hate and fear within which Black women, children and men have to survive. These analyses also help us to see how whiteness continues to construct itself as a racialized gender position *in opposition* to Blackness while attempting to remain invisible as the normative position of superiority within 'post-race' coloniality. Analyses of Black representation also help us to see how we are implicated, how we continue to be interpellated by Western Hemispheric anti-Blackness and, therefore, why the images that we live with and through matter for Black feminist decolonial social/theoretical/political/identification/social justice transformation. However, transformation is not pain-free, and its possibility is depleted by the violence and trauma of the afterlife of enslavement (Hartman, 1997, 2016; Sexton, 2011, 2018; Sharpe, 2010, 2016; Wilderson 111, 2010, 2020). Anti-Black intersectional racism and its attendant unfreedom have no apparent expiration date.

The 2020 racist murder of George Floyd in the US led to the Democrats drawing up anti-lynching legislation as Black communities spoke about feeling like they were 'being hunted'. After initial failure, the Emmett Till Bill was passed by the US Senate in March 2022 (Pengelly, 2022). Imagine, in the 21st-century US, anti-lynching legislation is necessary! The use of 'lynching' made clear that the #BlackLivesMatter's 'I can't breathe' and 'No justice, no peace' was a 21st-century protest against a colonial and contemporary history of state-sanctioned violence against Black women, men and children. Up to the point of Floyd's death and indeed beyond it, the police could and can continue to kill with impunity.

Of course, any student of race and racism would say that this points to the continuation of the violence, pain and trauma of the plantation within Western Hemispheric democratic states. This means that Black lives are still being lived within the power structures of coloniality and this is becoming ever more visible. Quoting Trinidadian American Black Panther Stokely Carmichael, Ornette D. Clennon (2018: 2) writes:

> If a white man wants to lynch me, that's his problem. If he's got the power to lynch me, that's my problem. Racism is not a question of attitude; it's a question of power. This question of power is about a system that confers privilege on whom it chooses to recognise [...] the system can arbitrarily make up rules as it goes along in order to maintain the status quo of privilege.

The question of white power and Butler's chokehold should not, indeed, *must not* be forgotten in contexts in which James Baldwin's assertion in *I Am Not Your Negro* (2017, Director Raoul Peck), 'You cannot lynch me or keep me in ghettos without becoming something monstrous yourselves', continues to be a necessary political provocation. Especially so, when Black bodies irrespective of gender, sexuality, class, ability and age, for example, are fungible, disposable (Hartman, 1997), precarious and ungrievable (Butler, 2004).

Using the discussion of 'the theft, regulation and destruction of black women's sexual and reproductive capacities', Saidiya Hartman (2016: 166) asserts that this also defines the afterlife of slavery. The afterlife of slavery resonates all over the Western Hemisphere and its long history of Black death, where Black women still live the 'wound dealt to [their] reputation as a human being' (Hartman, 2016: 166). We see this in the police shooting and paralysis of Cherry Groce in 1985 in the UK. Her shooting sparked the 1985 Brixton uprising and she died in 2011 from kidney failure linked to the gunshot injury. We see this in the police shooting death of Breonna Taylor in 2020 in the US, whose name was held up in the #BLM marches. We see this in Marielle Franco, a Black lesbian left-wing councillor in Rio de Janeiro, Brazil, who was shot to death at the age of 38 in March 2018 with her driver Anderson Gomes, in an apparently carefully targeted murder by professionals. Tens of thousands of people took to the streets across Brazil over her murder which sent Brazilians searching for answers to questions about racism, violence and the impunity of killers like hers. Franco was a women's, single mothers' and gay rights campaigner, who spoke out against the violence of the police against favela residents and collusion with the drug gangs and unofficial militias (theguardian.com Observer Dispatch 'Marielle Franco: Brazil's Favelas Mourn the Death of a Champion', Dom Phillips, Saturday March 17, 2018). Although separated by the Atlantic Ocean and decades, these incidents show the continuing precarity of Black lives in anti-Black necropolitical states such as the UK, USA and Brazil.

The condition of the enslaved mother means that Black communities 'carry the mother's mark and it continues to define our condition and our present' (Hartman, 2016: 167). Further, within the carceral landscape of the plantation the 'fungibility of the slave, the wanton uses of the black body for producing value or pleasure, and the shared vulnerabilities of the commodity, whether male or female, trouble dominant accounts of gender' (Hartman, 2016: 167). Indeed, Black enslaved women's reproductive labour 'guaranteed slavery as an institutional process and secured the status of the enslaved [through *partus sequitur ventrem*], but it inaugurated a regime of racialized sexuality that continues to place black bodies at risk for sexual exploitation and abuse, gratuitous violence, incarceration, poverty, premature death, and state-sanctioned murder' (Hartman, 2016: 168). There has been too much Black death, whilst Black life continues to be lived with and through pain.

What does it mean to live with and through pain? This was a question which many of us meditated on during the Covid-19 pandemic in 2020–2022 in the midst of escalating Black deaths and the summer of the #BlackLivesMatter Movement in 2020 following George Floyd's death. Being 'hunted and killed' in the US because of skin and its systemic injustices means politically and existentially that Black life still continues not to matter *as life*. Black skin is wrapped in an existential crisis. The previous examples show that this existential crisis emerges because Black women, men and children inhabit and survive within necropolitical (Mbembe, 2019) states all over the Black Atlantic. Necropolitical life is an inescapable certainty within the Black Atlantic because of its racialized gender skin politics embedded within anti-Black hate.

Anti-Black hate is a technology of terror produced through a cycle of pain as affective, physical and feared. This technology of terror results in pain's performative production of peculiar individualizations and segmentations of *skin as flesh* as we see rendered in representations and death on the streets. Pain is amplified through a crisis induced by fear. Fear of the possibility of visitation of terror on and in the individual and communal body, such that Black pain and suffering increases the terror of pain itself. Although we saw the shareability of Black pain in the worldwide #BLM 2020, the pain of anti-Black hate is also individualized, unshareable in its very shareability through communal grief (Tate and Wahidin, 2013). Indeed, 'the unshareability of pain ruptures […] attachments to the world; to have pain is to lose (materials for) one's self, to be emptied of a self' because of the 'fracturing of the connections that make [them] into something, that give [them] "ontological security"' (Fournier, 2002: 64). Psychic pain seeps into sentient skin and back again in an endless cycle as pain unmakes the self because that pain potentially 'brings […] the hatred for a self that has been engulfed by and reduced to an abject body' (Fournier, 2002: 66).

Giving in to what Lorde (2007a) calls un-metabolized pain leads to total annihilation, the reduction to an abject body and as all links are cut to that which gives meaning to the self, to ontological insecurity. Instead of this, Lorde (2007a) asks that we recognize the pain felt, the anger experienced and use it to build community through affect such as joy. Frank Wilderson 111 also speaks to Lorde's erotic politics of community building when he says, '[T]he affective side of Afro-pessimism is important for giving critical recognition to Black rage for your existence, your capacity to be Human, and not just your actions' (Wilderson 111 and King, 2020: 57). Pain, terror, anger enable agency as we *read into* fugitivity/maroonage/errantry, as we *read into* freedom.

Freedom is not yet a given, even though we can be lulled into a false sense of security that it is already here through events which might seem to be inclusive of Blackness or even attempts at antiracism by state, institution, business or individual. For example, in January 2022, Maya Angelou became the first African American woman to have her image on the US American quarter and UK *Vogue* had its first Black cover with darker-skinned models. For example, Naomi Campbell appeared with her baby daughter on the March 2022 cover of British *Vogue* with a stunning long natural hair wig, and Ketanji Brown Jackson was named as President Biden's pick to serve on the US Supreme Court. We can see these as progress in terms of Black representation, but surely we should also ask the question – why did this take so long? We also have to remember that Black women are leaders in all areas of socio-economic and political life in other parts of the world and that does not receive the same amount of attention. Also, why is it that these are so very exceptional as to draw comment, not on their beauty, artistic merit or talent *but on their inclusion as exceptions*? What now lies ahead as culture wars against being 'woke', intersectionality and critical race studies being taught in universities and schools and the right to engage in antiracist decolonial protest continue to rage in Europe and the US since 2020? These examples amongst others should make us remember that Black freedom has still not been won. It has still got to be fought for.

Glossary

Affect A 'dimension of life – including of writing [and] reading – which directly carries a political valence [...] for thinking through the intensities of feeling that fill life and form it' (Massumi, 2015: vii). Feelings 'become affects, circulating in encounters [...] and mutually recreating our relational bonds and (dis)attachments' (Gutiérrez Rodríguez, 2010: 4).

Afropessimism A theoretical understanding of racial enslavement, race and anti-Blackness shape the Afropessimist theoretical lens situating relations of power. '[...It] is a critical project [...] deploying Blackness as a lens of interpretation, [to] interrogate Marxism, postcolonialism, psychoanalysis, and feminism through rigorous consideration of their [...] foundations, methods, form, and utility. [...] It is pessimistic about the claims theories of liberation make when [they ...] explain Black suffering. [...] Afropessimism argues *Blacks are not Human subjects, but are instead structurally inert props, implements for the execution of White and non-Black fantasies and sado-masochistic pleasures*' (Wilderson, 2020).

Beauty 'Beauty is political. It is the prize claimed by the victors of struggles over human worth. The sting of ugliness is a weapon used by those at the top of social hierarchies to assert superiority over groups they deem inferior and therefore ugly. [...] Beauty politics are gender politics [...] the extent to which beauty defines women

remains greater [than men] [...] and because gender is
always co-constructed with race and class, beauty politics
are racialized, classed, gender politics' (Craig, 2022: 3).
'Black beauty is [...] performative and [...] an ongoing
negotiation of aesthetics, stylization technologies, feminist
and anti-racist/ Black Nationalist ideology in the Black
Atlantic diaspora' (Tate, 2009: 1).

Fascination 'Fascinate in its original Latin was '*fascinare*'
[...] to bewitch. If you fascinate someone you irresisti-
bly attract their interest, their desire [...] even if they find
what they are looking at repellent. [...] Fascination exerts
an inter-corporeal connectedness even when we feel fear,
disgust, contempt. [... In] fascination [...] comparisons
are made to the norm' (Tate, 2015a: 94).

Fear 'Black consciousness is feared in antiblack societies [...]
fear [...] leads to disrespect for truth, and antipathy to the
ethical and political implications of admitting that truth,
[...] the realization of what is [...] revealed about claims of
white supremacy and black inferiority [...] seen through
the eyes of Blacks. That revelation is [...the] lies on which
the [...] legitimacy of antiblack societies is built [...] what
is feared is what one may learn about oneself, the image of
oneself that might emerge' (Gordon, 2022: 20, 25).

Pan-Africanism '[...T]here has never been one univer-
sally accepted definition of exactly what constitutes Pan-
Africanism. [...M]ost writers would agree that the phenomenon has emerged in the modern period and is con-
cerned with the social, economic, cultural and political
emancipation of African peoples, including those of the
African diaspora [... and] the belief in the unity, common
history and common purpose of the peoples of Africa
and the African diaspora and the belief that their desti-
nies are interconnected [...] many would [also] highlight
the importance of the liberation and advancement of the
African continent itself' (Adi, 2018: 2).

Post-race/post-racial The idea that contemporary liberal
democracies have transcended race and racism. Racism
is not systemic, structural, populist or institutional, and

it is only individual shortcomings that explain inequality. While time has been called on racism, structurally, institutionally and systemically racism rages on. Goldberg (2015) claims that the post-racial is the basis of contemporary racisms. The 'post'-race illusion forms contemporary racial structures.

Racializing assemblages Used to discuss how race as sociopolitical processes divide people into full humans, not-quite-humans and nonhumans. Alexander Weheliye (2014: 1–2, 6) develops the idea of 'racializing assemblages of subjection' to 'understand the workings of and abolish our extremely uneven global power structures defined by the intersections of neoliberal capitalism, racism, settler colonialism, immigration, and imperialism, which interact in the creation and maintenance of systems of domination; and dispossession, criminalization, expropriation, exploitation, and violence that are predicated upon hierarchies of racialized, gendered, sexualized, economized, and nationalized social existence […] race, racialization, and racial identities [are] ongoing sets of political relations that require, through constant perpetuation via institutions, discourses, practices, desires, infrastructures, languages, technologies, sciences, economics, dreams, and cultural artefacts, the barring of non-white subjects from the category of the human as it is performed in the modern west […] racializing assemblages represent, among other things, the visual modalities in which dehumanization is practiced and lived'.

Racism 'No black or Indigenous person [or Person of Colour] is discriminated against *as an individual*. Antiblack racism is against *blacks*. Anti-Indigenous racism is against *Indigenous peoples* [anti-People of Colour racism is against *People of Colour*]' (Gordon, 2022: 13). Racism is structural, systemic, institutional and interpersonal and based on the ideology of race as biology.

Bibliography

Adi, H. (2018) *Pan-Africanism: A history*. London: Bloomsbury Academic.

Ahmed, S. (1999) '"She'll wake up one of these days and find she's turned into a nigger": Passing through hybridity', *Theory Culture and Society*, 16(2), pp. 87–106.

Ahmed, S. (2014) *The cultural politics of emotion*. Edinburgh: Edinburgh University Press.

Aldrich, R. (2002) *Colonialism and homosexuality*. New York/London: Routledge.

Alexander, M.J. (2006) *Pedagogies of crossing: Meditations on feminism, sexual politics, memory, and the sacred*. Durham: Duke University Press.

Alexander, M.J. and Mohanty, C.T. (1997) 'Introduction: Genealogies, legacies, movements', in Alexander, M.J. and Mohanty, C.T. (eds.) *Feminist genealogies, colonial legacies, democratic futures*. New York/London: Routledge, pp. xiv–xliii.

Alexander-Floyd, N. (2012) 'Disappearing acts: Reclaiming intersectionality in the social sciences in a post-Black feminist era', *Feminist Formations*, 24(1), pp. 1–25.

Ali, S. (2003) *Mixed–race, post-race: Gender, new ethnicities and cultural practices*. London: Berg.

Anzieu, D. (1990) *The skin ego*, trans. Chris Turner. New Haven: Yale University Press.

Aspers, P. and Godart, F. (2013) 'Sociology of fashion: Order and change', *Annual Review of Sociology*, 39, pp. 171–192.

Bailey, M. and Trudy (2018) 'On misogynoir: Citation, erasure and plagiarism', *Feminist Media Studies*, 18(4), pp. 762–768.

Banet-Weiser, S. (1999) *The most beautiful girl in the world: Beauty pageants and national identity*. Berkeley/Los Angeles/London: University of California Press.

Banks, I. (2000) *Hair matters: Beauty, power, and Black women's conscious-ness*. New York and London: New York University Press.

Barnes, N. (1994) 'Face of the nation: Race, nationalisms and identi-ties in Jamaican beauty pageants', *The Massachusetts Review*, 35(3/4), Autumn, pp. 471–492.

Bell, P., Smith, B and Hull, G (1982) *All the women are white, all the men are Black, but some of us are brave*. New York: The Feminist Press.

Bhabha, H. (1990) 'The third space: Interview with Homi Bhabha', in Rutherford, J. (ed.) *Identity, community, culture, difference*. London: Lawrence and Wishart, pp. 207–221.

Bilge, S. (2020) 'The fungibility of intersectionality: An Afro-pessimist reading', *Ethnic and Racial Studies*, 43(13), pp. 2298–2326.

Blumer, H. (1969) 'Fashion: From class differentiation to collective selection', *Sociological Quarterly*, 10, pp. 275–291.

Bonilla-Silva, E. (2010) *Racism without racists: Color-blind racism and the persistence of racial inequality in America*. Plymouth: Rowman and Littlefield.

Bordo, S. (2000) 'Beauty discovers the male body', in Ziglin Brand, P. (ed.) *Beauty matters*. Bloomington and Indianapolis: Indiana University Press, pp. 112–153.

Bourdieu, P. (1987) *Distinction: A social critique of the judgement of taste*. Cambridge, MA: Harvard University Press.

Bourdieu, P. (2021) *Forms of capital: General sociology volume 3: Lectures at the Collège de France 1983–84*. Cambridge: Polity Press.

Brennan, T. (2014) *The transmission of affect*. Ithaca, NY: Cornell University Press.

Briggs, A. (2013) 'Capitalism's favourite child: The production of fashion', in Bruzzi, S. and Gibson, P. (eds.) *Fashion cultures*. London/New York: Routledge, pp. 186–199.

Brown, J. (2008) *Babylon girls: Black women performers and the shaping of the modern*. Durham: Duke University Press.

Brown-Glaude, W. (2007) 'The fact of Blackness? The bleached body in contemporary Jamaica', *Small Axe*, 24(3), October, pp. 34–51.

Bryan, B. Dadzie, S. and Scafe, S., eds., (1985/2018) *The heart of the race: Black women's lives in Britain*. London: Verso.

Buscaglia-Salgado, J. (2003) *Undoing empire: Race and nation in the mulatto Caribbean*. Minneapolis: University of Minnesota Press.

Butler, J. (2004) *Precarious life: The powers of mourning and violence*. London: Verso.

Butler, P. (2017) *Chokehold: Policing black men*. New York: The New Press.

Campion, K. (2019) '"You think you're Black?' Exploring mixed-race experiences of Black rejection', *Ethnic and Racial Studies*, 42(16), pp. 196–213.

Candelario, G. (2007) *Black behind the ears: Dominican racial identity from museums to beauty shops*. Durham: Duke University Press.

Carby, H. (1982) 'White women listen! Black feminism and the boundaries of sisterhood' in Centre for Contemporary Cultural Studies (eds.) *The Empire Strikes Back: Race and Racism in 70's Britain*. London/New York: Routledge, pp. 211–234.

Carby, H. (1987) 'White woman listen! Black feminism and the boundaries of sisterhood', in Mirza, H.S. (ed.) *Black British feminism: A reader*. London/New York: Routledge, pp 45–53.

Carby, H. (2007) 'Postcolonial translations', *Ethnic and Racial Studies*, 30(2), pp. 213–234.

Carr, R. (2002) *Black nationalism in the new world: Reading the African–American and West Indian experience*. Durham: Duke University Press.

CBC News (2019) 'What we know about Justin Trudeau's blackface photos-and what happens next', *cbc.ca*, 26 September 2019. Available at: https://www.cbc.ca/news/canada/toronto/tdsb-parkdale-blackface-petition-1.6232252 (Accessed 12 November 2021).

Centre for Contemporary Cultural Studies (1982) *The empire strikes back: Race and racism in 70's Britain*. London: Hutchinson with the Centre for Contemporary Cultural Studies.

Césaire, A. (2000) *Discourse on colonialism*, trans. J. Pinkham. New York: Monthly Review Press.

Cheddie, J. (2010) 'Troubling subcultural theories on race, gender, the street, and resistance', *Fashion Theory: The Journal of Dress, Body & Culture*, 14(3), September, pp. 331–354.

Cheng, A.A. (2011) *Second skin: Josephine Baker and the modern surface*. Oxford: Oxford University Press.

Christian, Mark (2008) 'The Fletcher report 1930: A historical case study of contested Black mixed heritage Britishness', *Journal of Historical Sociology*, 21(2/3), June/September, pp. 213–241.

Clennon, O.D. (2018) *Black scholarly activism between the academy and grassroots: A bridge for identities and social justice*. Cham, Switzerland: Palgrave Macmillan.

Coard, S. and Breland, A. (2001) Perceptions of and preferences for skin color, Black racial identity and self-esteem among African Americans, *Journal of Applied Social Psychology*, 31(11), pp. 2256–2274.

Collins, P.H. (1990/2022) *Black feminist thought: Knowledge, consciousness and the politics of empowerment*. New York/London: Routledge 30th Anniversary Edition.

Collins, P.H. (2019) *Intersectionality as critical theory*. Durham: Duke University Press.

Collins, P.H. and Bilge, S. (2020) *Intersectionality*, 2nd edn. Cambridge, UK: Polity Press.

Cooper, C. (2010) 'Caribbean fashion week: Remodeling beauty in "Out of Many One" Jamaica', *Fashion Theory: The Journal of Dress, Body & Culture*, 14(3), pp. 387–404.

Craig, M.L. (2022) 'Introduction', in Craig, M.L. (ed.) *The Routledge companion to beauty politics*. London/New York: Routledge, pp. 3–9.

Craik, J. (1993) *The face of fashion: Cultural studies of fashion*. London: Routledge.

Crenshaw, K. (1989) 'Demarginalizing the intersection of race and sex: A Black feminist critique of antidiscrimination doctrine, feminist theory and antiracist politics', *University of Chicago Legal Forum*, 1, Article 8. http://chicagounbound.uchicago.edu/uclf/vol1989/iss1/8.

Crenshaw, K. (1991) 'Mapping the margins: Intersectionality, identity politics and violence against women of color', *Stanford Law Review*, 43(6), pp. 1241–1299. https://doi.org/10.2307/1229039

Curiel, O. (2016) 'Rethinking radical antiracist feminist politics in a global neoliberal context', *Meridians*, 14(2), pp. 46–55.

Curry, T. (2017) *The man-not: Race, class, genre and the dilemmas of Black manhood*. Philadelphia, Pennsylvania: Temple University Press.

Curry, T. (2021) 'Foreword: Black maleness as a deleterious category', in Kitossa, T. (ed.) *Appealing because he is appalling: Black masculinities, colonialism and erotic racism*. Edmonton: University of Alberta Press.

Davis, A. (1983) *Women, race and class*. New York: Vintage Books.

Davis, A. (1994) 'Afro images: Politics, fashion and nostalgia', *Critical Inquiry*, 21(1), Autumn, pp. 37–45.

Davis, K. and Evans, M., eds., (2016) *Transatlantic conversations: Feminism as travelling theory*. London/New York: Routledge.

Derrida, Jacques (2005) *The politics of friendship*, trans. George Collins. London: Verso.

Di Angelo, R. (2019) *White fragility: Why it's so hard for white people to talk about racism*. London: Penguin.

Dosekun, S. (2016) 'Editorial: The politics of fashion and beauty in Africa', *Feminist Africa* 21, pp. 1–6.

Dosekun, S. (2020) *Fashioning postfeminism: Spectacular femininity and transnational culture*. Urbana, Chicago, and Springfield: University of Illinois Press.

Edwards, T. (2011) *Fashion in focus: Concepts, practices and politics*. London: Routledge.

Elam, M. (2011) *The souls of mixed folks: Race, politics and aesthetics in the new millennium*. Stanford: Stanford University Press.

Elliott, R. (2020) ''The fantasy of purity is appalling': Deconstructing identify in the human stain', *Philip Roth Studies*, 16(1), Spring, pp. 92–110.

Espinosa Miñoso, Y. (2007) *Escritos de una lesbiana oscura: Reflexiones críticas sobre el feminismo y política de identidad en América Latina*. Buenos Aires and Lima: En La Frontera.

Espinosa Miñoso, Y. (2019) 'Doing genealogy of experience: Towards a critique of the coloniality of feminist reason derived from the historical experience in Latin America', *Direito e Práxis*, 10(3), pp. 2007–2032.

Fanon, F. (2001) *The wretched of the earth*. London: Penguin Classics.

Fanon, F. (2021) *Black skin. White masks*. London: Penguin Classics.

Foucault, M. (1975) *Discipline and punish: The birth of the prison*, trans. by Alan Sheridan. London: Penguin Books.

Foucault, M. (1980) *The history of sexuality volume 1: An introduction*, trans. Robert Hurley. New York: Vintage, Random House.

Foucault, M. (1980b) *Power/knowledge: Selected interview and other writings, 1972–1977*. New York: Random House.

Foucault, M. (1995) *The birth of biopolitics: Lectures at the Collège de France 1978–1979*, trans. G. Burchell. Basingstoke/New York: Palgrave Macmillan.

Fournier, V. (2002) 'Fleshing out gender: Crafting gender identities on women's bodies', *Body and Society*, 8(2), pp. 55–77.

Freud, S. (2016 originally published 1905) *Three essays on the theory of sexuality*, trans. U. Kistner, P. Van Haute and H. Westerink. London: Verso.

Gardner, S. and Hughey, M. (2017) 'Still the tragic mulatto? Manufacturing multiracialism in magazine media 1961–2011', *Ethnic and Racial Studies*, 42(4), pp. 645–665.

Garvey, M. (1923) 'An expose of the caste system among negroes', in Garvey, A.J., ed. (1968) *The philosophy and opinions of Marcus Garvey*. London/New York: Routledge, pp. 68–74.

Gilligan, S. (2012) Fragmenting the Black male body: Will Smith, masculinity, clothing, and desire', *Fashion Theory: The Journal of Dress, Body & Culture*, 16(2), pp. 171–192.

Gilman, S. (1985) *Difference and pathology: Stereotypes of sexuality, race and madness*. Ithaca/London: Cornell University Press.

Gilman, S. (1992) *The Jew's body*. New York/London: Routledge.

Gilroy, Paul (2004) *After empire: Melancholia or convivial culture?* London: Routledge.

Glissant, E. (1997) *Poetics of relation*, trans. Betsy Wing. Ann Arbor: University of Michigan Press.

Goldberg, D.T. (2015) *Are we all postracial yet?* Cambridge, UK: Polity Press.

Goldson, R.R. (2020) 'Liberating the mind: Rastafari and the theorization of maroonage as epistemological (dis)engagement', *Journal of Black Studies*, 51(4), May, pp. 368–385.

Goldthree, R.N. and Duncan, N. (2018) 'Feminist histories of the interwar Caribbean: Anti-colonialism, popular protest, and the gendered struggle for rights', *Caribbean Review of Gender Studies*, 12, pp. 1–30.

Gordon, L.R. (1997) *Her majesty's other children: Sketches of racism from a neo-colonial age.* Oxford: Rowman and Littlefield.

Gordon, L.R. (2014) 'On the monstrous threat of reasoned Black desire', in Michlin, M. and Rocchi, J.-P. (eds.) *Black intersectionalities: A critique for the twenty first century.* Liverpool Scholarship Online. https://doi.org/10.5949/Liverpool/9781846319389.003.0012

Gordon, L.R. (2022) *Fear of Black consciousness.* London: Penguin.

Gubar, S. (1997) *Racechanges: White skin, Black face in American culture.* New York/Oxford: Oxford University Press.

Gutiérrez Rodríguez, E. (2010) *Migration, domestic work and affect: A decolonial approach on value and the feminization of labor.* New York/Abingdon, Oxon: Routledge.

Hadreas, P. (2007) *A phenomenology of love and hate.* Aldershot: Ashgate.

Hall, J.C. (2017) 'No longer invisible: Understanding the psychosocial impact of skin color stratification in the lives of African American women', *Health and Social Work*, 42(2), pp. 71–78.

Hall, R. (2015) 'Dark skin, Black men and colorism in Missouri-Murder vis-à-vis psychological icons of Western masculinity', *Spectrum: A Journal of Black Men*, 3(2), pp. 27–43.

Hall, S. (1997) 'The spectacle of the 'other'', in Hall, S. (ed.) *Representation and signifying practices.* London: Sage Publications/The Open University, pp. 279–283.

Hall, S (1996a) 'Introduction – Who needs identity?', in Hall, S. and du Gay, P. (eds.) *Questions of cultural identity.* London: Sage, pp. 1–17.

Hall, S. (1996b) 'What is this Black in Black popular culture?', in Morley, D. and Chen, K-H (eds.) *Stuart Hall – Critical dialogues in cultural studies.* London: Routledge, pp. 465–475.

Hartman, S (1997) *Scenes of subjection: Terror, slavery, and self-making in nineteenth-century America.* Oxford/New York: Oxford University Press.

Hartman, S. (2016) 'The belly of the world: A note on Black women's labors', *Souls: A Critical Journal of Black Politics, Culture and Society*, 18(1), pp. 166–173.

Hesse, B. (2014) 'Escaping liberty: Western hegemony, Black fugitivity', *Political Theory*, 42(3), June, pp. 288–313.

Hobson, J. (2005) *Venus in the dark: Blackness and beauty in popular culture.* New York: Routledge.

Hobson, J. (2018) *Venus in the dark: Blackness and beauty in popular culture*, 2nd edn. New York: Routledge.

Hodge-Freeman, E. (2013) 'What's love got to do with it? Racial features, stigma and socialization in Afro-Brazilian families', *Ethnic and Racial Studies*, 36(10), Special Issue Rethinking Race, Racism, Identity and Ideology in Latin America, pp. 1507–1523.

Holmes, S. and Redmond, S. (2006) 'Introduction: Understanding celebrity culture', in Holmes, S. and Redmond, S. (eds.) *Framing celebrity: New directions in celebrity culture*, London: Routledge, pp. 1–16.

hooks, b. (1981) *Ain't I a woman? Black woman and feminism.* London/New York: Routledge.

hooks, b. (2003) *We real cool: Black men and masculinity.* New York/London: Routledge.

hooks, b. (2014) *Black looks: Race and representation*, 2nd edn. New York/London: Routledge.

Hope, D. (2010) *Man vibes: Masculinities in the Jamaican dancehall.* Kingston and Miami: Ian Randle.

Hope, D. (2009) Fashion ova style: Contemporary notions of skin bleaching in Jamaican dancehall culture. *JENdA: A Journal of Culture and African Women's Studies*, 14, pp. 101–126.

Hosein, G. and Outar, L., eds. (2016) *Indo-Caribbean feminist thought: Genealogies, theories, enactments.* Cham, Switzerland: Palgrave Macmillan.

Hosten, J. (2008) *Beyond Miss World* (with Shaun Sarsfeld). St. Michael, Barbados: Cole's Printery.

Hosten, J. (2020) *Miss World 1970: How I entered a beauty pageant and wound up making history.* Toronto: Sutherland House.

Houston, M. G. (2012) *Ancient Egyptian, Mesopotamian and Persian costume.* Mineola, NY: Dover.

Howard, P.S.S. (2018) 'A laugh for the national project: Contemporary Canadian blackface humour and its constitution through Canadian anti-Blackness', *Ethnicities*, 18(6), pp. 843–868. https://doi.org/101177/1468796818785936

Hua, M. (2011) *Chinese clothing*. Cambridge, UK: Cambridge University Press.

Hunter, M. (2005) *Race, gender and the politics of skin tone*. London/New York: Routledge.

Hunter, M. (2021) 'Colorism and the racial politics of beauty', in Leeds Craig, M. (ed.) *The Routledge companion to beauty politics*. London/New York: Routledge, pp. 85–93.

Hyam, R. (1991) *Empire and sexuality: The British experience*. Manchester, UK: Manchester University Press.

Ifekwunigwe, J. (1999) *Scattered belongings: Cultural paradoxes of "Race", nation and gender*. London: Routledge.

Jackson, R. (2006). *Scripting the Black masculine body: Identity, discourse and racial politics in popular media*. Albany: SUNY Press.

Jackson, S. (2012) *Creole Indigeneity: Between myth and nation in the Caribbean*. Minneapolis: University of Minnesota Press.

Jarrett-Macauley, D. (2009) *The life of Una Marson, 1905–65*. Manchester: Manchester University Press.

Johnson, J. (2016) 'Usain Bolt beating classism and racism in Jamaica', *The Gleaner*, 25 January. Available at: https://jamaica-gleaner.com/article/news/20160125/usain-bolt-beating-classism-and-racism-jamaica (Accessed 24 January 2022).

Johnson, T. (2020) *Innocent subjects: Feminism and whiteness*. London: Pluto Press.

Kelley, R. (1997) 'Nap time: Historicizing the Afro', *Fashion Theory: The Journal of Dress, Body & Culture*, 1(4), pp. 339–351.

Kelly, R.D. (2000) 'Introduction: A poetics of anti-colonialism', *Césaire*, 2000, pp. 7–28.

King, T.L. (2019) *The black shoals: Offshore formations of Black and Native studies*. Durham: Duke University Press.

Kitossa, T. (2021) 'Can the Black man be nude in a culture that imagines him as naked? A Baldwinian and Fanonian psychosexual reading of black masculinity in 'Western' art and cinema', in Kitossa, T. (ed.) *Appealing because he is appalling: Black masculinities, colonialism and erotic racism*. Edmonton: University of Alberta Press, pp. 3–58.

Kondo, D. (2003) 'Dorinne Kondo in interview with Nirmal Puwar', *Fashion Theory: The Journal of Dress, Body & Culture*, 7(4), pp. 253–256.

Kondo, D. (1997) *About face: Performing race in fashion and theater*. London: Routledge.

Kuipers, G., Chow, Y. F. and van der Laan, E. (2014) 'Vogue and the possibility of cosmopolitics: Race, health and cosmopolitan engagement in the global beauty industry', *Ethnic and Racial Studies*, 37(12), pp. 2158–2175.

Kuryloski, L. (2019) 'Black wimmin who pass, pass into damnation: Race, gender and the passing tradition in Fannie Hurst's *Imitation of Life* and Douglas Sirk's film adaptation', *Journal of Narrative Theory*, 49(1), Winter, pp. 27–52.

Lafrance, M. (2018) 'Skin studies', *Past, Present and Future, Body and Society*, March. https://doi.org/10.1177/1357034X18763065

Law, I. (2010) *Racism and ethnicity*. London: Routledge.

Law, I. (2014) *Mediterranean racisms, connections and complexities in the Mediterranean region*. Basingstoke: Palgrave.

Laybourn, W.M. (2017) 'The cost of being 'real': Black authenticity, colourism and Billboard rap chart rankings', *Ethnic and Racial Studies*, 41(11), pp. 2085–2103.

Lewis, G. (2013) 'Unsafe travel: Experiencing intersectionality and feminist displacement', *Signs: Journal of Women in Culture and Society*, 38(4), Special Issue Intersectionality: Theorizing Power and Empowering Theory, Cho, S., Crenshaw, K. and McCall, L. (ed.) pp. 869–892.

Lewis, G (2005) 'Welcome to the margins: Diversity, tolerance, and politics of exclusion', *Ethnic and Racial Studies*, 28(3), pp. 536–558.

Lhamon Jr. W.T. (1989) 'Chuck Berry and the sambo strategy in the 1950s', *Studies in Popular Culture*, 12(2), pp. 20–29.

Lorde, A. (2007a) 'Uses of the erotic: The erotic as power', in *Sister outsider: Essays and speeches*. New York: Random House, pp. 53–59 (originally published 1984, Trumansburg, NY: Crossing Press).

Lorde, A. (2007b) 'The master's tools will never dismantle the master's house', in *Sister outsider: Essays and Speeches*. Berkeley, California: Crossing Press, pp. 110–113.

Lott, E. (1991) 'The seeming counterfeit: Racial politics and early blackface minstrelsy', *American Quarterly*, 43(2), June, pp. 223–254.

Lott, E. (1993) *Love and theft: Blackface minstrelsy and the American working class*. Oxford: Oxford University Press.

Marsen, U. (1937) 'Kinky hair blues', in Marsen, U. edited by Donnell, A. (2011) *Selected Poems*. Leeds: Peepal Tree Press, pp. 144–145.

Massumi, B. (2015) *Politics of affect*. Cambridge, UK: Polity Press.

Mbembe, A. (2019) *Necropolitics*. Durham: Duke University Press.

McClintock, A. (1995) *Imperial leather: Race, gender, and sexuality in the colonial contest*. New York/London: Routledge.

McCracken, A. (2014) *The beauty trade: Youth, gender and fashion globalization*. Oxford: Oxford University Press.

McMillan, M. (2017) Saga bwoys, rude bwoys and saggers: Rebellious Black masculinities', *Critical Arts*. https://doi.org/10.1080/02560046.2017.13834921

Mears, A. (2011) *Pricing beauty: The making of a fashion model*. Oakland, CA: University of California Press.

Mercer, K. (1994) *Welcome to the jungle: New positions in Black cultural studies*. London/New York: Routledge.

Mills, C. (1997) *The racial contract*. Ithaca: Cornell University Press.

Mills, C. (2007) 'White ignorance', in Sullivan, S. and Tuana, N. (eds.) *Race and epistemologies of ignorance*. Albany: State University of New York Press. pp.

Mirza, H.S., ed. (1997) *Black British feminism: A reader*. London/New York: Routledge.

Mirza, H.S. (2022) ' 'A vindication of the rights of black women': Black British feminism then and now', in Tate, S.A. and Gutiérrez Rodríguez, E. (eds.) *The Palgrave handbook on critical race and gender*. Cham, Switzerland: Palgrave Macmillan, pp. 189–207.

Mohammed, P. (2002) 'Introduction: The material of gender', in Mohammed, P. (ed.) *Gendered realities: Essays in Caribbean feminist thought*. Mona, Jamaica: University of the West Indies Press.

Mohammed, P. (2000) '"But most of all mi love me browning": The emergence in eighteenth and nineteenth century Jamaica of the mulatto woman as desired', *Feminist Review*, 65, Summer, pp. 22–48.

Mohapatra, R.P. (1992) *Fashion styles of ancient India: A study of Kalinga from earliest times to sixteenth century AD*. Gurugram, India: South Asia Books.

Monk, E.P. (2019) 'The color of punishment: African Americans, skin tone and the criminal justice system', *Ethnic and Racial Studies*, 42(10), pp. 1593–1612.

Morrison, T. (1994) *Playing in the dark: Whiteness and the literary imagination*. New York: Vintage Books.

Moten, F. (2018) *Consent not to be a single being: Stolen life*. Durham: Duke University Press.

Nama, A. (2011) *Super black: American pop culture and Black superheroes*. Austin: University of Texas Press.

Nash, J. (2018) *Black feminism reimagined: After intersectionality*. Durham: Duke University Press.

Nash, J. (2020) 'Practicing love: Black feminism, love-politics, and post-intersectionality', *Meridians: Feminism, Race, Transnationalism*, 19(3), pp. 439–462. https://doi.org/10.1215/15366936-8566089

Ngai, S. (2005) *Ugly feelings*. London: Harvard University Press.

Norwood, K.J., ed. (2014) Color matters: Skin tone bias and the myth of a post-racial America. New York/London: Routledge.

Obregon, E. (2020) 'Así son los cubanos: Narratives of race and ancestry', *Ethnic and Racial Studies*. https://doi.org/10.1080/01419870.2020.1823447

Olumide, J. (2002) *Raiding the gene pool: The social construction of mixed race*. London: Pluto Press.

Ortega, M. and Lugones, M. (2020) 'Carnal disruptions: Mariana Ortega interviews María Lugones', in Dipieto, P.J., McWeeny, J. and Roshanravan, S. (eds.) *Speaking face to face: The visionary philosophy of Maria Lugones*. Albany: State University of New York Press.

Oyewúmì, O. (1997) *The invention of women: Making an African sense of western gender discourses*. Minneapolis: University of Minnesota Press.

Park, L. (2020) '"Afropessimism and futures of…" A conversation with Frank Wilderson', *Journal of Black Studies and Research*, 50(3), Special Issue: What Was Black Studies? Pp. 29–41.

Pateman, C. and Mills, C. (2007) *Contract and domination*. Cambridge, UK: Polity.

Patterson, O. (1982) *Slavery and social death: A comparative study*. Cambridge, MA: Harvard University Press.

Pengelly, M. (2022) 'US Senate unanimously passes bill to make lynching a federal hate crime', *Guardian*, 8 March 2022. Available at: https://www.theguardian.com/world/2022/mar/08/us-senate-unanimously-passes-bill-to-make-lynching-a-federal-hate?CMP=Share_iOSApp_Other (Accessed 3 August 2022).

Perry, B. (2004) 'A crime by any other name: The semantics of hate', *Journal of Hate Studies*, 4, pp. 121–136.

Phillips, T. Trevor's at it again. Intermix. Available at: http://www.intermix.org.uk/news/news_310107_01.asp. (Accessed 28 October 2016).

Phizacklea, A. (1990) *Unpacking the fashion industry: Gender, racism and class in production*. New York/London: Routledge.

Potts, C. and Johnson, E. (2020) 'Complexion and phenotype in Portland, Oregon', *Spectrum: A Journal on Black Men*, 8(1), Fall, pp. 87–109.

Povinelli, E. A. (2006) *The empire of love: Towards a theory of intimacy, genealogy and carnality*. Durham: Duke University Press.

Prosser, J. (1998) *Second skins: The body narratives of transsexuality*. New York: Columbia University Press.

Reddock, R. (2007) 'Gender equality, Pan-Africanism and the diaspora', *International Journal of African Renaissance Studies-Multi-, Inter- and Transdisciplinary*, 2(2), pp. 255–267.

Reddock, R. (2007a) 'Diversity, difference and Caribbean feminism: The challenge of anti-racism', *Caribbean Review of Gender Studies*, 1, pp. 1–24.

Reddock, R. (2022) 'Pan-Africanism and feminism in the early twentieth century British colonial Caribbean', in Tate, S.A. and Gutiérrez Rodríguez, E. (eds.) *The Palgrave handbook of critical race and gender*. Cham, Switzerland: Palgrave Macmillan, pp. 143–166.

Reece, R. L. (2020) 'The gender of colorism: Understanding the intersection of skin tone and gender inequality' *Journal of Economics, Race, and Policy*, 4 pp. 47–55 https://doi.org/10.1007/s41996-020-00054-1

Regester, C.B. (2010) *African American actresses: The struggle for visibility, 1900–1960*. Bloomington, IN: Indiana University Press.

Reuters (2022) 'Dreams of Rio animate Ivory Coast's Popo Carnival', 6 May. (Accessed 12 March 2022).

Roberts, D.E. (2011) *Fatal invention: How science, politics and big business re-create race in the twenty-first century*. New York/London: The New Press.

Robinson, C. (2019) *Cedric J. Robinson: On racial capitalism, Black internationalism and cultures of resistance*, Ed. H.L.T. Quan. London: Pluto Press.

Robinson, C. (2021) *Black Marxism: The making of the Black radical tradition*. London: Penguin Classics.

Roediger, D.R. (1999) *The wages of whiteness: Race and the making of the American working class*. London: Verso.

Rooks, N.M. (2000) *Hair raising: Beauty, culture and African American women*. Piscataway, NJ: Rutgers University Press.

Roth, P. (2000) *The human stain*. New York: Vintage.

Rowe, R. (2009) 'Glorifying the Jamaican girl: The "Ten Types One People" beauty contest, racialized femininities and Jamaican nationalism', *Radical History Review*. https://doi.org/10.1215/01636545-2008-039

Rowe, R. (2013) *Imagining Caribbean womanhood: Race, nation and beauty competitions 1929–70*. Manchester: Manchester University Press.

Russell, K., Wilson, M. and Hall, R. (1992) *The color complex: The politics of skin color among African Americans*. New York: Doubleday.

Sandoval, C. (2000) *Methodology of the oppressed*. Minneapolis/London: University of Minnesota Press.

Schreiber, F. (2021) 'Movement: Dandies: The Sapeurs are countering Congolese misery with a merciless sense of style', *TANZ*, 2, February, p. 5.

Scott, D. (2010) *Extravagant abjection: Blackness, power and sexuality in the African American literary imagination*. Albany, New York: New York University Press.

Seigworth, G. and Gregg, M. (2010) 'An inventory of shimmers', in Seigworth, G. and Gregg, M. (eds.) *The affect theory reader*. Durham: Duke University Press, pp. 1–25.

Sexton, J. (2011) 'The social life of social death: On Afro-pessimism and Black optimism', *InTensions Journal*, 5, Fall/Winter, ISSN #1913–5874.

Sexton, J. (2018) *Black Men, Black feminism: Lucifer's nocturne*. Cham, Switzerland: Palgrave Macmillan.

Sharpe, C. (2010) *Monstrous intimacies: Making post-slavery subjects*. Durham: Duke University Press.

Sharpe, C. (2016) *In the wake: On Blackness and being*. Durham: Duke University Press.

Sharpley-Whiting, T.B. (2007) *Pimps up, ho's down: Hip hop's hold on young Black women*. New York: New York University Press.

Sherwood, M. (2000) *Claudia Jones: A life in exile*. London: Lawrence and Wishart.

Simmel, G. (1957) 'Fashion', *The American Journal of Sociology*, 62 (6), pp. 541–558.

Soja, E. (1996) *Third space: Journeys to Los Angeles and other real-and-imagined places*. Oxford: Wiley.

Spillers, H.J. (2003) 'Mama's baby, papa's maybe: An American grammar book', *Diacritics*, 17 (2), pp. 64–81.

Spivak (1990) 'Can the subaltern speak?' in Williams, P. and Chapman, L. (eds.) *Colonial discourse and postcolonial theory – A reader*. New York: Simon and Schuster Group, Hemel Hempstead, pp. 66–111.

Stephens, M. (2014) *Skin acts: Psychoanalysis and the Black male performer*. Durham: Duke University Press.

Stewart, K. (2007) *Ordinary affects*. Durham: Duke University Press.

Stockhill, C. and Carson, G. (2021) 'Are lighter skinned Tanisha and Jamal worth more pay? White people's gendered colorism toward Black applicants with racialized names', *Ethnic and Racial Studies*. https://doi.org/10.1080/01419870.2021.1900584

Stoler, A. L. (1995) *Race and the education of desire: Foucault's history of sexuality and the colonial order of things*. Durham: Duke University Press.

Stoler, A. L. (2002) *Carnal knowledge and imperial power: Race and the intimate in colonial rule*. Berkley: University of California Press.

Sudbury, J. (1998) *Other kinds of dreams: Black women's organizations and the politics of transformation*. New York/London: Routledge.

Sullivan, S. and Tuana, N. (2007) 'Introduction', in Sullivan, Shannon and Tuana, Nancy (eds.) *Race and epistemologies of ignorance*. Albany: State University of New York Press, pp. 1–2.

Tate, S.A. (2005) *Black skins Black masks: Hybridity, dialogism, performativity*. Aldershot: Ashgate.

Tate, S.A. (2007) 'Black beauty: Shade, hair and anti-racist aesthetics', *Ethnic and Racial Studies*, 30(2), pp. 300–319.

Tate, S.A. (2009) *Black beauty: Aesthetics, stylization, politics*. London/New York: Routledge.

Tate S.A. (2010) 'Not all the women want to be white: decolonizing beauty studies', in Gutiérrex Rodríguez, E., Boatca, M. and Costa, S. (eds.) *Decolonizing European sociology: Transdisciplinary approaches*. London/New York: Routledge.

Tate, S.A. (2012) 'Michelle Obama's arms: Race, respectability and class privilege', *Comparative American Studies*. https://doi.org/10.1179/1477570012Z.00000000017 Corpus ID: 144148065

Tate, S.A. (2015a) *Black women's bodies and the nation: Race, gender and culture*. NY/Basingstoke, UK: Palgrave Macmillan.

Tate, S.A. (2015b) 'Performativity and raced bodies', in Murji, K. and Solomos, J. (eds.) *Theories of race and ethnicity: Contemporary debates and perspectives*. Cambridge: Cambridge University Press, pp. 180–197.

Tate, S.A. (2016) *Skin bleaching in Black Atlantic zones: Shade shifters*. New York: Palgrave Macmillan.

Tate, S.A. (2016a) 'A tale of two Olympians', in Irvin, S. (ed.) *Body aesthetics*. Oxford: Oxford University Press. https://doi.org/10.1093/acprof:oso/9780198716778.003.0006

Tate, S.A. (2016b) *Black beauty: Aesthetics, stylization, politics*. New York, NY/London: Routledge.

Tate, S.A. (2017a) *The governmentality of Black beauty shame: Discourse, iconicity and resistance*. London: Palgrave Macmillan.

Tate, S.A. (2017b) 'Libidinal economies of Black hair: Subverting the governance of strands, subjectivities and politics', *Image and Text*, 29, pp. 95–111.

Tate, S.A. (2019) 'The dark skin I live in: Decolonizing racial capitalism's aesthetic hierarchies in the diaspora', *Caribbean Review of Gender Studies – A Journal of Caribbean Perspectives in Gender and Feminism*, 13, pp. 173–198.

Tate, S.A. (2020a) 'On "brick walls" and other Black decolonial feminist dilemmas: Anger and racial diversity in universities', in Crul, M., Dick, L., Ghorashi, H. and Valenzuela, A. Jr (eds.) *Scholarly engagement and decolonisation: Views from South Africa, The Netherlands and the United States*. African Sun Media Book Series on Higher Education Transformation, Volume 1, 2020. https://doi.org/10.18820/9781928314578/03

Tate, S.A. (2020b) *Decolonising sambo: Transculturation, fungibility and Black and People of Colour futurity*. Bingley: Emerald Books.

Tate, S.A. (2021) '"I do not see myself as anything else than white': Black resistance to racial cosplay/blackfishing', in Craig, M.L. (ed.) *The Routledge companion to beauty politics*. New York/London: Routledge, pp. 205–214.

Tate, S.A. and Law, I. (2015) *Caribbean racisms: Connections and complexities in the Caribbean region*. Basingstoke, UK: Palgrave MacMillan.

Tate, S.A. and Wahidin, A. (2013) 'Extraneare: Pain, loneliness and the incarcerated female body', *Illness, Crisis and Loss*, 21(3), August, pp. 203–217.

Taylor, P. (2000) 'Malcolm's conk and Danto's colors: Or four logical petitions concerning race, beauty, aesthetics', in Brand, P. (ed.) *Beauty matters*. Bloomington: Indiana University Press.

Telles, E. (2006) *Race in another America: The significance of skin color in Brazil*. Princeton, NJ: Princeton University Press.

Thomas, D. (2004) *Modern Blackness: Nationalism, globalization and the politics of culture in Jamaica*. Durham: Duke University Press.

Thomas, G. (2016) '*Marronnons*/Let's maroon: Sylvia Wynter's 'Black metamorphosis' as a species of maroonage', *Small Axe: A Caribbean Journal of Criticism*, 49, March, pp. 62–78.

Thompson, D. (2009) Racial ideas and gendered intimacies: the regulation of interracial relationships in North America. *Social and Legal Studies*, 18(3), https://doi.org/10.117/096466390933988

Tice, K.W. (2021) 'Beauty pageants and border crossings: The politics of class, cosmopolitanism, race and place', in Leeds Craig, M. (ed.) *The Routledge companion to beauty politics*. London/New York: Routledge, pp. 316–325.

Truillot, M.-R. (2015) *Silencing the past: Power and the production of history*. MA: Beacon Press.

Tsri, K. (2016) *Africans are not black: The case for conceptual liberation.* London/New York: Routledge.

Tulloch, C. (1998) '"Out of many, one people": The relativity of dress, race and ethnicity to Jamaica, 1880–1907', *Fashion Theory*, 2(4), pp. 359–382.

Vergès, F. (2021) *A decolonial feminism*, trans. Ashley J. Bohrer with the author. London: Pluto Press.

Walcott, R. (2018) 'Freedom now suite: Black feminist turns of voice', *Small Axe: A Caribbean Journal of Criticism*, 22(3), November, pp. 151–159.

Walther, C.S. (2014) 'Skin tone, biracial stratification and triracial stratification among sperm donors', *Ethnic and Racial Studies.* https://doi.org/10.1080/01419870.2012.696666

Watt, D. and Jones, A.D. (2015) *Catching hell and doing well-Black women in the UK: Abasindi Co-operative.* London: Trentham Books and the Institute of Education.

Weaver, S. (2010) 'Developing a rhetorical analysis of racist humour: Examining anti-Black jokes on the internet', *Social Semiotics*, 20(5), November, pp. 537–555.

Weheliye, A. (2014) *Habeas viscus: Racializing assemblages, biopolitics, and Black feminist theories of the human.* Durham: Duke University Press.

Wekker, G. (2016) *White innocence: Paradoxes of colonialism and race.* Durham: Duke University Press.

Wilder, J. (2010) 'Revisiting 'color names and color notions': A contemporary examination of the language and attitudes of skin color among young Black women', *Journal of Black Studies*, 41 (1), pp. 184–206. https://doi.org/10.1177/0021934709337986

Wilder, J. (2015) *Color stories: Black women and colorism in the 21st century.* Santa Barbara, CA/Denver, CO: Praeger.

Wilderson 111, F. (2020) *Afropessimism.* New York: Liveright Publishing.

Wilderson 111, F. (2010) *Red, white and Black: Cinema and the structure of U.S. antagonisms.* Durham: Duke University Press.

Wilderson 111, F. and King, T.L. (2020) 'Staying ready for Black study: A conversation', in King, T.L., Navarro, J. and Smith, A. (eds.) *Otherwise worlds: Against settler colonialism and anti-Blackness.* Durham: Duke University Press.

Williams, R. (1977) *Marxism and literature.* Oxford: Oxford University Press.

Wilson, A. (1978) *Finding a voice: Asian women in Britain*, (2nd edn.). 2018. Daraja Press. Kindle Edition.

Wingard, J. (2017) *Branded bodies, rhetoric, and the neoliberal nation-state.* London/New York: Rowman and Littlefield.

Woodard, V. (2014) *The delectable Negro: Human consumption and homo-eroticism within US slave culture.* New York/London: New York University Press.

Wynter, S. (1979) 'Sambos and minstrels', *Social Text*, 1, Winter, pp. 146–156.

Wynter, S. (1994) '"No humans involved": An open letter to my colleagues'. Forum N.H.I.: Knowledge for the 21st century, 1 (1), Fall, pp. 1–17.

Wynter, S. (1996) '1492: A new world view', in Lawrence Hyatt, V. and Nettleford, R. (eds.) *Race, discourse and the Americas: A new world view.* Washington, DC: Smithsonian Institution Press, pp. 6–57.

Wynter, S. (2003) 'Unsettling the coloniality of being/power/truth/freedom: Towards the human after man, its overrepresentation – an argument', *CR New Centennial Review*, 3(93), Fall, pp. 257–337.

Yancy, G. (2008) *Black bodies white gazes: The continuing significance of race.* Lanham, MD: Rowman and Littlefield Publishers.

Yancy, G. (2012) *Look a white! Philosophical essays on whiteness.* Philadelphia, PA: Temple University Press.

Young, L. (1996) *Fear of the dark: 'Race', gender and sexuality in cinema.* London/New York: Routledge

Yuen, N.W. (2017) *Reel inequality: Hollywood actors and racism.* New Brunswick, NJ: Rutgers University Press.

Zack, Naomi (1993) *Race and mixed race.* Philadelphia: Temple University Press.

Zaidi, T. (2020) *Sapeurs: Ladies and gentlemen of the Congo.* Germany: Kehrer.

Index

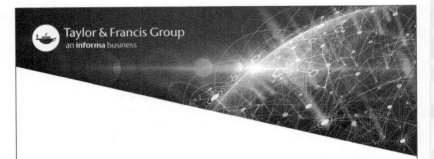

For Product Safety Concerns and Information please contact our EU
representative GPSR@taylorandfrancis.com Taylor & Francis Verlag GmbH,
Kaufingerstraße 24, 80331 München, Germany

Printed and bound by CPI Group (UK) Ltd, Croydon, CR0 4YY
08/06/2025
01897000-0002